THE CAPITAL MARKET EFFECTS OF INTERNATIONAL ACCOUNTING DIVERSITY

THE CAPITAL MARKET EFFECTS OF INTERNATIONAL ACCOUNTING DIVERSITY

Frederick D.S. Choi
New York University

Richard M. Levich
New York University
National Bureau of
Economic Research

Dow Jones-Irwin
Homewood, Illinois 60430

This publication is designed to provide accurate and
authoritative information in regard to the subject matter
covered. It is sold with the understanding that neither the
author nor the publisher is engaged in rendering legal, accounting,
or other professional service. If legal advice or other expert
assistance is required, the services of a competent
professional person should be sought.

*From a Declaration of Principles jointly adopted by a Committee
of the American Bar Association and a Committee of Publishers.*

Project editor: Karen Nelson
Production manager: Carma W. Fazio
Jacket design: Sam Concialdi
Compositor: Eastern Graphics Typographers
Typeface: 11/13 Times Roman
Printer: Arcata Graphics/Kingsport

Library of Congress Cataloging-in-Publication Data

Choi, Frederick D.S.
    The capital market effects of international accounting diversity /
Frederick D.S. Choi, Richard M. Levich.
        p.   cm.
    Includes bibliographical references.
    ISBN 1-55623-429-5
    1. Accounting.   2. Capital market.   3. Investments, Foreign.
I. Levich, Richard M.   II. Title.
HF5657.C542   1990
657'.76—dc20   90–3240
                                                    CIP

Printed in the United States of America
1 2 3 4 5 6 7 8 9 0   K   7 6 5 4 3 2 1 0

PREFACE

There has been a tremendous surge in global trading activity in the last few years, and it is broadly expected that this growth in international capital markets activity will continue. Market participants—investors, corporate issuers, investment underwriters, and market regulators— must contend with a host of complexities when investment activities extend beyond national boundaries, not the least of which is the need to deal with accouting statements that reflect different traditions of accounting and corporate reporting. While considerable attention has been given in academic and professional activities to the identification of diverse accounting principles in various countries, little work has been devoted to the important question of whether such differences actually have an impact on international capital market activity. Examination of the literature and previous discussions with colleagues in academe and representatives of the business world have provided little in the way of hard data. This study is a modest attempt to fill that void and is, we believe, the first study of its kind to marshal empirical evidence on this important and interesting question.

This research project was funded by a grant to the Stern School of Business from Arthur Andersen & Co. and Salomon Brothers Incorporated. We wish to thank Philip Peller, J. Matthew Singleton, Arthur Wyatt, and their colleagues at Arthur Andersen & Co., Michael Frinquelli and colleagues at Salomon Brothers Incorporated, and our colleagues Edward Altman, John Bildersee, Ernest Bloch, Joshua Ronen, Arnold Sametz, Roy Smith, and Ingo Walter of the Stern School of Business for helpful comments and suggestions received at various stages of the research. We also express our gratitude to Jonathan Bloomer, Andreas Burge, Helmut Schmekel, and Richard Wroten of Arthur Andersen & Co. for their assistance at our non-U.S. interview sites. We especially thank Yasuo Shimizu of Arthur Andersen & Co. for serving as our translator in Tokyo. Above all we wish to thank all of the capital market participants we interviewed for sharing their views with us. Their willing cooperation helped to make this study possible. The analysis and conclusions expressed herein are those of the authors and do not necessarily reflect the views of the participating organizations. The authors accept responsibility for any errors that remain.

Frederick D.S. Choi
Richard M. Levich

CONTENTS

LIST OF TABLES

LIST OF EXHIBITS

OVERVIEW

In the dynamic world of commerce and finance, the only constant is change itself. While business has operated internationally for some time, recent developments require a heightened international perspective on the part of decision makers. As examples:

1. A reinvigorated European Community has targeted December 31, 1992, as the date by which barriers to the harmonization of product, factor, and financial markets will be removed.
2. Political developments in Eastern Europe signal a disenchantment with communism and greater acceptance of capitalist values.
3. Foreign investors are more visibly and aggressively investing directly in U.S. companies and properties.
4. Capitalizing on the growing trend of national governments to deregulate their capital markets and recent advances in computer and telecommunications technology, institutional investors are increasingly looking to overseas equities as an avenue to enhance investment performance.
5. It is no longer the large, well-known multinationals that are doing business and financing their external capital needs abroad. Credit and investment analysts must increasingly look to foreign accounts for information on earnings and growth prospects for lesser-known companies.

Accounting, as the language of business, is very much a part of the changing business scene. Financial decisions are made daily by individuals who rely, directly or indirectly, on accounting information. If that information is inconsistent with underlying economic events or is misunderstood, resultant decisions may be less than optimal. There is today a growing concern among participants in international capital markets about whether accounting rules are in synchronization with underlying economic fundamentals. Some argue, for example, that the price-to-earnings ratios of Japanese shares are relatively high because the economic prospects of Japanese firms are better. They argue that the cost of funds in Japan is lower or that earnings growth patterns are superior because of productive efficiencies and product quality. Others argue that the *economics* of Japanese firms are not necessarily better. Rather, higher P/E ratios in Japan may be driven either by purely speculative factors or by factors germane to this study—namely, accounting distortions.

If accounting measurement rules were the only difference among countries, then—assuming adequate data—straightforward transformation of the figures (analogous to converting feet or yards to their metric equivalents) would be sufficient to enable accounting reports to be universally understood and interpreted unambiguously. Unfortunately, countries also exhibit substantial economic and cultural differences that preclude accounting figures from having the same interpretation, even if they were generated using the same accounting principles.

What are the implications of international accounting differences for different users or preparers of accounting statements? For *investors*, there is the issue of the comparability of investment prospects where enterprise performance is measured under different accounting rules. Are investors able to sort out those differences in financial measures of risk and return that are a function of (*a*) accounting principles differences, (*b*) economic or cultural differences, or (*c*) real differences in the attributes being measured? For corporate *issuers*, there is the increasingly complex decision of where to raise capital and how to minimize associated costs. Are issuers able to communicate clearly without distorting the intended messages for foreign investors who are accustomed to providing capital on the basis of financial statements prepared according to differing languages, currencies, and accounting frameworks? For *capital market regulators*, policies must be set for accounting and reporting principles for foreign entities that seek to issue or list their shares in the regulator's home country. Are regulators able to resolve the many tradeoffs between investor protection issues and demands on foreign firms with well-developed traditions of accounting? Insistence on reporting norms that differ from those of the reporting entity's country-of-domicile may cause foreign issuers to access another capital market. On the other hand, accommodation to foreign issuers must take into account competing information needs of domestic investors and the desirability of maintaining a level playing field with domestic issuers.

Because of these and related issues, there is a growing interest in efforts to harmonize international accounting standards. In our view, progress toward harmonized standards may continue to be slow and the benefits of any new policy uncertain in the absence of empirical evidence as to whether, and in what specific ways, accounting diversity affects capital market decisions. Specifically, for whom is international accounting diversity a problem, and what is the precise nature of those problems? Does the juxtaposition of international financial decisions and divergent national accounting principles lead to problems of understanding and interpretation by foreign statement readers? How do users attempt to cope with accounting diversity? Are their coping mechanisms successful or do problems remain? Do problems caused by accounting diversity lead to capital market effects? If so, what is the nature of those effects? Finally, would international accounting standards yield positive benefits? Are uniform accounting standards really necessary for the efficient functioning of international capital markets?

To answer these questions, we gathered information directly from capital market participants. Specifically, we interviewed institutional investors, corporate issuers, underwriters, market regulators, and other capital market participants in Japan, Switzerland, the United Kingdom, the United States, and West Germany using a structured, but open-ended interview format.

What did we find? Overall, one half of those queried feel that their capital market decisions are affected by accounting diversity. This finding understates the proportion of users who feel that accounting differences matter, as it does not include second-order behavioral effects—for example, users who changed the way in which they analyze investments in foreign markets. For those whose decisions are affected by accounting differences, diversity is often associated with capital market effects. These effects relate to the geographic location of market activity, the types of companies invested in, types of securities issued, information processing costs, and the pricing of international securities.

Response patterns, however, are not uniform, either within respondent groups or between respondent groups. More than one half of the institutional investors interviewed feel that accounting differences hinder the measurement of their decision variables and ultimately affect their investment decisions. Investors respond to accounting differences with various forms of coping behavior. A significant number of investors cope by restating foreign accounting numbers to the reporting principles of the investor's country-of-domicile or to a set of accounting principles that are internationally recognized. Restatement, however, does not appear sufficient to remove the problem of accounting diversity. This suggests that existing restatement algorithms may not be optimal, are not being applied effectively, or are incapable of producing meaningful information.

Some investors rely on original accounting statements and a well-developed knowledge of foreign accounting practices and financial market conditions. These investors with multiple principles capabilities (MPC), while small in number, report no decision problems or capital markets effects. Some of these investors even feel that they profit from their special or scarce capabilities. On the other hand, some of those who report not being affected by accounting diversity may not be coping in optimal fashion, implying that their investment performance may be substandard.

Investors appear evenly divided as to the necessity or utility of international accounting standards. Those in favor of international standards feel that harmonization will not only make analysts' lives easier but will enlarge investor interest in international markets.

Most issuers do not feel that differences in accounting measurement rules affect their decisions. On the other hand, disclosure differences appear to have an impact on financing decisions, suggesting that accounting diversity and regulatory diversity are closely linked issues. Large issuers with extensive experience in international finance appear to experience fewer problems caused by accounting differences. While there are exceptions, it appears that small or relatively inexperienced firms that are venturing into the international capital markets stand to benefit from advice on how to effectively deal with such differences. Nationality also seems to play a role in explaining issuer behavior. U.S. and U.K. firms, whose standards of accounting and financial disclosure tend to be relatively high, appear to have greater flexibility in accessing international capital markets. On the other hand, German, Japanese, and Swiss firms appear to have less flexibility.

Issuers' problems with accounting diversity, however, may also be related to the asymmetry we observe between the United States and other countries in our sample with regard to financial market regulation.

Other countries embrace reciprocity in accepting accounting and reporting practices of the issuer's home country. This may explain why no
American firms in our sample felt accounting issues raised difficulties
for them in tapping international capital markets. In contrast, the United
States insists on national treatment (i.e., restatement or reconciliation to
U.S. GAAP and U.S.-style disclosure) for public issues or listed securities. This posture imposes additional costs on non-U.S. issuers, and
some are not willing to bear these costs.

All firms in our sample seek to minimize their funding costs. To
better understand corporate funding behavior, we find it useful to model
a firm's cost of capital in a broad context as a function of (1) financial
costs, (2) information preparation costs, and (3) competitive costs. This
framework is helpful in explaining the corporate decision effects of accounting diversity and observed coping behavior. Country of origin also
plays a role in our model of total cost minimization. Issuers from a
country with substantial accounting disclosure will be more concerned
about the impact of GAAP differences on their competitive costs. Issuers from a country with limited disclosure requirements tend to be
more concerned about the competitive costs of additional disclosure.

Based on the observed coping behavior of various corporate issuers, it appears that some non-U.S. firms have avoided problems related to accounting diversity by reason of their size, name recognition,
their ability to generate funds internally, or by the good fortune of being
"grandfathered" into the U.S. market.

Demand for international accounting standards does not seem to be
emanating from the corporate world. In view of the multiple constituen
cies with which a company must cope, compliance with international
standards would impose an added variable to the decision calculus of
financial managers.

Accounting diversity is regarded as a problem by most of the underwriters in our sample. This is a problem, in turn, that is associated
with capital market effects ranging from the geographic scope of their
underwriting activities to the pricing of international issues.

The responses of underwriters more than likely reflect those of
their clients. Underwriters will likely approach a variety of investors,
some of whom will be more or less interested in accounting data and
more or less adept at dealing with them in original or restated terms.
Similarly, underwriters will represent issuers from numerous countries
who are more or less comfortable providing a range of accounting data

and disclosures. As financial intermediaries between borrowers and lenders, underwriters must adapt to the decision needs of their clientele. National market regulators in the countries surveyed do not appear hindered by accounting differences in making their regulatory decisions. Nevertheless, extremes in regulatory disclosure requirements can have adverse effects on the location of market activity and, therefore, market growth. Accordingly, the issue of identifying an optimum disclosure framework for international corporate issuers or listers is an important consideration among some regulators.

The demand for harmonized accounting standards does not seem to be emanating from most of the market regulators we surveyed. Many regulators prefer alternatives to those being advanced by the International Accounting Standards Committee (IASC). Support for international standards stems not so much from the adverse effects of accounting diversity on regulatory decision processes as it does from the competitive market for regulation.

Our overall conclusion in the policy area is that policy prescriptions regarding international accounting must be based on empirical evidence. Our finding that many investors believe they cope successfully and that many issuers have elected to depart from U.S. or IASC practices suggests that many market participants do not anticipate private benefits from alternative accounting rules and disclosure arrangements. Whether any set of harmonized international accounting standards will improve social welfare remains an unanswered question. The welfare distributional effects suggest that it will be difficult to reach a consensus on uniform international accounting policies.

Based on the paradigm that accounting rules should be consistent with environmental norms—economic, cultural, institutional—national accounting rules would be similar only to the extent that environmental systems (including tax policy, fiscal policy, regulatory objectives, managerial systems, performance incentives, and other cultural factors) were broadly similar across countries. The diversity in the manufacturing and service corporate sectors as seen against the backdrop of diverse national economic, cultural, and institutional settings begs the question of whether the necessary conditions are in place to recommend a uniform international accounting system.

CHAPTER 1

INTRODUCTION

OVERVIEW OF ENVIRONMENTAL FACTORS

Owing to international linkages of commodity prices, interest rates, and currency exchange values, governments around the world are supporting initiatives to coordinate national policies. In recent years these initiatives have embraced such areas as trade policy, fiscal and monetary policy, banking regulation, and rules governing the operation and structure of financial markets.

A closely related development in the world of finance is the internationalization of securities markets. Encouraged by recent advances in telecommunications and the gradual deregulation of national capital markets, domestic investors are expanding their purchases of foreign debt and equity securities. In 1988, U.S. gross purchases and sales of foreign stocks exceeded $140 billion, a ninefold increase over the flows reported in 1982. Foreigner gross purchases and sales of U.S. stocks exceeded $380 billion, a fivefold increase over the same time span.[1] Motivating investor behavior are enhanced returns that are frequently available abroad, as well as the opportunity to reduce portfolio risk by diversifying internationally.[2] In similar fashion, business enterprises interested in increasing the supply and reducing the cost of capital are

---

[1] U.S. Government Accounting Office, *International Finance: Regulation of International Securities Markets* (Washington, D.C.: GAO, 1989), pp. 9–10.

[2] The first empirical demonstration of international diversification gains is attributed to Herbert G. Grubel, "International Diversified Portfolios: Welfare Gains and Capital Flows," *American Economic Review* 58 (1968), pp. 1299–1314. An up-to-date treatment of the literature on international investing is presented in Bruno Solnik, *International Investments* (Reading, Mass.: Addison-Wesley Publishing 1988).

increasingly sourcing their external financing needs abroad, in terms of both new issues and listings on foreign stock exchanges. As a result of these activities, funding and investment decisions have become international in scope.

However, accounting and financial reporting practices have not kept pace with these developments. In contrast to the developments noted above, the measurement and disclosure principles that underlie financial statement preparation have remained largely a nationalistic affair. When accounting reports retain a nationalistic character, it is reasonable to fear that problems of understanding and interpretation may develop outside the country in which the reports are prepared. Apparent differences in financial measures of enterprise risk and return characteristics could be due as much to differences in accounting measurement rules as they are to real differences in the attributes being measured. If accounting measurement rules were the only difference among countries, then straightforward transformation of the figures (analogous to converting temperatures from Fahrenheit to centigrade or converting distances from miles to kilometers) would be sufficient to enable accounting reports, assuming sufficient data were available to users to make the desired adjustments, to be universally understood and interpreted unambiguously. Unfortunately, countries also reflect substantial economic and cultural differences that preclude accounting figures from having the same interpretation, even if they were generated using the same accounting principles. For example, a debt-equity ratio of 2.0 might suggest a highly levered and risky firm in the United States. In Japan, throughout most of the 1970s, a debt-equity ratio of 2.0 would not have been unusual, and might have been explained by the close linkages between Japanese firms and their debt holders.[3] Similarly, tax rules differ markedly across countries, and managers may be driven to push certain accounting entries in opposite directions simply to maximize their after-tax results. If these cultural and economic differences are substantial, a simple restatement of foreign accounting reports according to domestic principles may not be sufficient for domestic readers to properly analyze foreign firms.

To put the matter succinctly, when the accounting measures for

---

[3]Given the tremendous rise in equity prices in Japan, debt-equity ratios in Japan are now only one-half as large as those for U.S. firms. See Kenneth French and James Poterba, "Are Japanese Stock Prices Too High?" manuscript, NBER Summer Institute, August 1989.

two firms are presented to a reader, can the reader determine whether observed differences are the result of (*a*) accounting measurement differences, (*b*) economic, cultural, and institutional differences across countries, or (*c*) real differences in the attributes being measured? In practice, this difficult problem is compounded by the fact that certain accounting data are not disclosed in some countries. And even where disclosures are similar, differences in auditing standards or practices may affect the reader's confidence in reported figures.

In the interest of resolving this reporting conundrum, and partly as an outgrowth of harmonization efforts at the macroeconomic level mentioned above, there is renewed interest today in achieving some form of global accounting harmony. Some might take the case for accounting harmony to be irrefutable. Like apple pie and motherhood, harmony and coordination of national accounting policies, they argue, can only promote economic welfare. In this view, the question is not whether we should have greater accounting harmony, but which approach should be taken. Suggested alternatives include the following:

1. Allow diversity in accounting treatments to continue, but require sufficient disclosure to enable statement readers to understand the nature and extent of the diversity and make appropriate adjustments.
2. Narrow the areas of difference in financial reporting by permitting a limited choice of accounting treatments but allowing freedom of choice within a narrow band.
3. Eliminate international accounting diversity by promulgating a single set of uniform accounting standards.
4. Permit hybrids of the foregoing options such as "primary-secondary" reporting, whereby a company supplements financial statements prepared according to local accounting norms with financial statements prepared according to international accounting standards.

MOTIVATION FOR THIS STUDY

In our view, the question of the optimal degree of accounting harmony is a complex empirical matter. Before setting off to do more costly and time consuming numerical estimates, however, we believe it is essential to ascertain whether, and to what extent, international accounting diversity is actually a problem.

Care must be taken to frame the issues properly. The question, for example, "Does international accounting diversity matter?" is not a well-formulated question. Accounting diversity always matters in the sense that the reader must know whether he is about to read financial statements prepared according to U.S., French, or Japanese accounting principles—exactly as anyone must know whether a temperature is being expressed in Farenheit or centigrade, whether a distance is in miles or kilometers, or whether a book is written in the English, French, or Japanese language. Once these parameters are known, the fact that some distances are expressed in miles and others in kilometers might have no effect on, for example, travel decisions.

A better series of questions begins instead by asking whether international accounting diversity is *important*, in that it affects economic or financial decisions. This basic question then leads us to ask whether the juxtaposition of international financial decisions and divergent accounting principles leads to problems of understanding and interpretation by users outside the reporting country. For whom is international accounting diversity a problem, and what is the precise nature of those problems? How do users attempt to cope with accounting diversity? Are existing coping mechanisms successful, or do problems remain? Do the problems lead to capital market effects? If so, what is the nature of those effects?

In the same manner, a question such as "Would the harmonization of international accounting standards be desirable?" is also not well-formulated. As one of our interview subjects told us, he was in favor of "motherhood and clean air, and against poverty and the man-eating shark." Naturally, world harmony along many dimensions would be welcome if they could be had for free. A better question to ask is "Would international accounting standards generate social benefits that exceed social costs?" Are international accounting standards really necessary for an efficiently functioning international capital market? Would international initiatives to harmonize global accounting standards offer a successful remedy to the transnational reporting problem?

One organization, the International Accounting Standards Committee (IASC), appears to have reached a conclusion on many of these issues. In their words:[4]

---

[4]See International Accounting Standards Committee, *Objectives and Procedures* (London: IASC, 1983), par. 3.

Investors in international markets need to be sure that the information on which they base their assessments is compiled using accounting principles recognized in their own country and comparable with others regardless of the country of origin. Interested groups, such as employees, government agencies and regulatory bodies will only find financial statements acceptable if they are based on standards which are relevant, balanced and internationally comparable.

The members of IASC believe that the adoption in their countries of International Accounting Standards together with disclosure of compliance will over the years have a significant impact. The quality of financial statements will be improved and there will be an increasing degree of comparability. The credibility and consequently the usefulness of financial statements will be enhanced throughout the world.

We cannot quarrel with the objective of enhancing the usefulness of financial statements or the notion that additional information (although costly to produce) would be valued by capital market participants.[5] Expressing favor with comparable accounting statements and additional information, however, side-steps the fundamental question: what type of information would market participants consider decision-relevant? Would harmonized and comparable accounting statements be considered useful? Have market professionals and institutional investors already developed the skills to analyze foreign firms irrespective of accounting differences?

In our opinion, if the world exhibits diversity, then it may be necessary for accounting principles also to have diversity. Environmental diversity must be understood and brought to light, rather than papered over or artificially removed. Information adds value as it helps readers understand the economic, behavioral, and cultural forces affecting managers and firms. Accounting principles that reveal these factors assist investors in making rational economic decisions.

---

[5]That risk and uncertainty have a negative effect on the welfare of capital market participants is a fundamental tenet of financial theory. In the context of financial theory, Stephen Brown extended this notion by demonstrating that since the decision maker works with estimated model parameters rather than their true values, an additional source of uncertainty is introduced ("The Effect of Estimation Risk on Capital Market Equilibrium," *Journal of Financial and Quantitative Analysis* 14, 1979, pp. 215–20). Parameter uncertainty can be viewed as a barrier to international investing. William H. Branson and Dwight M. Jaffe analyze the implications of the quality of information on international capital mobility and welfare ("The Globalization of Information and Capital Mobility," working paper, New York University, Vincent C. Ross Institute of Accounting Research, September 15, 1989).

Seen in this light, the diagnosis and the prescription offered by the IASC are premature. Little is known as to whether, and to what extent, international accounting diversity is a problem. Accounting diversity has not been an insurmountable barrier—despite accounting diversity, the international dimension of capital markets has grown and attracted more participants. Several European stock exchanges (London, Frankfurt, and Zurich) each host several hundred foreign firms. It is currently estimated that, worldwide, at least one equity trade in nine has a foreign investor on the other side. As of year-end 1988, 6.7 percent of world equity market capitalization was held by cross-border investors.[6] Borrowers from around the world have issued more than \$1 trillion of debt in the Eurobond market over the last 20 years. Clearly, capital market participants have attempted to cope with accounting diversity. With the rapid development of international financial transactions, it is not obvious that accounting diversity *per se* has been a serious deterrent to growth in these markets. Still, accounting diversity may have reduced the amount of international financial transactions or adversely affected pricing relative to some optimal system.

Before a policy prescription can be rendered, several key questions must be addressed. First, a policy prescription to alter the status quo presumes that accounting diversity represents a cost to society. A policy prescription presumes further that the impact of the policy can be predicted and that the benefits of the policy outweigh the costs of imposing it. In our judgment, the research literature has yet to provide adequate evidence on even the first of these questions.

APPROACH TO THE STUDY

Quantification of the relationship between accounting diversity and capital market decisions is difficult in the absence of information on the relevant issues and variables that lend themselves to measurement. Accordingly, our attempt to ascertain the capital market effects of international accounting diversity will proceed in two phases. The purpose of

---

[6]Michael Howell and Angela Cozzini, *International Equity Flows—1989 Edition* (London: Salomon Brothers, 1989).

phase one, contained in this report, is to determine directly from the major users and providers of international accounting information (namely, investors in, and corporate issuers of, international securities) whether, and to what extent, differences in accounting principles, financial disclosure, and auditing practices affect the measurement of their decision variables and, ultimately, their financial decisions. We also explore the effects of accounting diversity on the location of market activity, market growth, the types of securities issued or invested in, information costs, and the pricing of international equities. As the decisions of both investors and issuers are typically made within the context of advice offered by financial intermediaries and guidelines enforced by national regulators, we also examine decision problems encountered by investment underwriters, debt-rating agencies, and national regulators.

In substantiating the nature and scope of problems caused by accounting differences, testimonials from active market participants will enable us to proceed to phase two of this inquiry. This phase will attempt to quantify in more rigorous fashion the capital market effects of international accounting diversity.

OVERVIEW OF CONCLUSIONS

The findings that we present here are based on interviews with representatives of 52 institutions headquartered in Japan, Switzerland, the United Kingdom, the United States, and West Germany. Overall, nearly one half of those in our sample feel that their capital market decisions are affected by accounting diversity. This finding is conservative, as it does not include second-order behavioral effects, that is, the many who responded, "We believe we are coping successfully (a behavioral change), hence our decisions are not affected." Therefore, we can reject the hypothesis that accounting diversity has no effect on capital market decisions. However, we also find differences in response patterns between groups and within groups. For example, some investors rely on original accounting statements and a well-developed knowledge of foreign accounting practices and financial market conditions. These investors with multiple principles capabilities (MPC) report no decision problems or capital market effects. Some of these investors even feel that they profit from their special or scarce capabilities. Similarly, many corporate issuers feel that accounting diversity is either not a difficult factor to cope with or not an important factor in the first instance. These firms do not feel that accounting diversity has affected their access to capital, its cost, or the market value of their shares. However, for those firms that cite accounting diversity as an important factor affecting their decisions, we note that these firms could have elected voluntarily to prepare and disclose additional accounting data in order to cope. That they do not suggests that some firms will be disadvantaged by rules requiring them to prepare and disclose accounting data they would not provide voluntarily.[7]

Our findings (that many investors believe they cope successfully and that many firms chose to depart from U.S. or IASC practices) suggest that it will be difficult to reach a consensus on uniform international accounting policies. Our findings also suggest that policy prescriptions in this area must be based on empirical evidence. Based on the premise that accounting rules should be consistent with environmental norms— economic, cultural, institutional—national accounting rules would be similar only to the extent that environmental systems (including tax policy, fiscal policy, regulatory objectives, managerial systems, performance incentives, and other cultural factors) were broadly similar across countries. The new supervisory guidelines for banking from the Bank for International Settlements are a good case in point. Now that policymakers have agreed to uniform guidelines for bank supervision (including capital adequacy measures and risk-rating measures), uniform accounting seems to be a natural outgrowth. In contrast, diversity in the manufacturing and service corporate sectors, as seen against the backdrop of diverse national economic, cultural, and institutional settings, begs the question of whether the necessary conditions are in place to recommend a uniform international accounting system.

Consider the case of Sweden. Swedish financial accounting and reporting practices are closely linked with national economic policies. The use of untaxed investment reserves is one instance of significant

---

[7]A study by G. K. Meek and S. J. Gray reports that some foreign firms listed on London's International Stock Exchange voluntarily provide disclosures beyond those required under the rules of the exchange ("Globalization of Stock Markets and Foreign Listing Requirements: Voluntary Disclosures by Continental European Companies Listed on the London Stock Exchange," *Journal of International Business Studies* 20, no. 2 [Summer 1989], pp. 315–36).

government subsidies to the business sector. This government-sanctioned charge against taxable income is partially funded in a noninterest bearing account with the Bank of Sweden and designed to encourage investment in depressed sectors of the economy to help smooth out the business cycle. To benefit from this incentive, corporate taxpayers availing themselves of this and other incentives must conform accounting income to taxable income. The reversal of untaxed reserves to conform to an international standard would risk making "unlike things appear alike."[8]

The remainder of this book is organized as follows. Chapter 2 contains background information on international accounting differences and financial market characteristics that form the basis for our principal research questions. Conventional wisdom on the capital market effects of accounting differences is contrasted with stylized empirical facts in Chapter 3. Our research methodology and survey design are described in Chapter 4. Findings of the study are detailed in Chapter 5. The major conclusions from the survey and implications for international capital market participants are highlighted in Chapters 6 and 7. Policy recommendations are set forth in Chapter 8. We conclude with an overview of suggestions for future research in Chapter 9.

---

[8]For a description of other tax-induced reserves in Swedish financial reporting, see F. D. S. Choi and G. G. Mueller, *International Accounting* (Englewood Cliffs, N.J.: Prentice Hall, 1984).

CHAPTER 2

DIVERSITY IN INTERNATIONAL FINANCIAL MARKETS AND ACCOUNTING

The focus of our research is on the linkages between international accounting practices and international capital markets. Before analyzing our survey findings on this topic, we present a brief overview of financial market characteristics around the world. We find national market features to be far from uniform. We also present a brief overview of accounting practices across countries to provide the reader with a sense of the variation.

DIVERSITY IN NATIONAL FINANCIAL MARKETS

In facilitating the transfer of capital from savers (investors) to enterprises (borrowers), financial markets fulfill an important role. Despite their commonality of purpose, world financial markets exhibit significant diversity in their operations, organization, and structure.

Summary statistics on major stock exchanges in Europe, Japan, and the United States are presented in Table 1.* Great disparities are evident in terms of market size (market capitalization), trading volume, and total number of listed firms. Japan and the United States stand out as the two largest countries in terms of market capitalization, followed by the United Kingdom, Canada, and Germany. While there is obviously some correlation between market size and the total number of

---

*Tables and Exhibits appear at the end of the text.

firms that are listed on local exchanges, there are some anomalies. There seems to be no correlation between market size and the number of foreign listings in a given country. The New York Stock Exchange (NYSE), has a market capitalization nearly 25 times as large as the Amsterdam Exchange. Yet there are only 77 foreign firms listed on the NYSE, while nearly three times that number are listed on the Amsterdam Exchange. In particular, there are virtually no German or French firms listed on the NYSE.[1] Similarly, on the Madrid, Milan, and Nordic exchanges, few if any foreign firms are listed.

In addition to these size and activity measures, stock markets differ in their organization and structural characteristics. The entries in Table 2 suggest how ownership, method of regulation, membership rules, price determination, and other features vary across markets. An important consideration in this study is variation in the listing fees and other requirements for foreign equities, as summarized in Table 3. Within the United States, the NYSE stands out as the most expensive in terms of fees, while those at NASDAQ appear trivial. Accordingly, over two thirds of the foreign securities listed in the United States are traded on NASDAQ. The Frankfurt Exchange stands out for requiring an issuer or lister to have a sponsoring bank. In our interviews in Germany, the importance of the sponsoring bank was stressed in vouching for the accounts and the character of the firm, as well as assuming legal liability. Sponsoring brokers play a similar role in other European and Asian markets.[2]

While it is generally observed that the same security (e.g., a share of IBM) sells for nearly the same price on two exchanges when adjusted by the spot foreign exchange rate, there is considerable question as to whether the same general pricing formula is used to price different shares on different markets.[3] Some statistics that can be measured, such as the Price/Earnings ratio (P/E), the Price/Cash Earnings ratio (P/C),

---

[1]List supplied by New York Stock Exchange, dated November 1, 1988.

[2]In the United States, sponsoring banks play a role in the administration of American Depositary Receipts (ADRs). For more information on ADR shares, see William E. Nix and Susan W. Nix, *The Dow Jones-Irwin Guide to International Securities, Futures, and Options Markets* (Homewood, Ill.: Dow Jones-Irwin, 1988).

[3]Evidence generally favorable to the Law of One Price for international securities is reported in Rita Maldonado-Bear and Anthony Saunders, "Foreign Exchange Restrictions and the Law of One Price," *Financial Management* 12, no. 1 (Spring 1983), pp. 19–23.

and the Price/Book Value ratio (P/B), reveal considerable variation across countries, as we see in Exhibits 1, 2, and 3. P/C measures are sometimes preferred, since cash earnings are less confounded by differences in accounting procedures, and in fact the coefficient of variation of P/C (0.43) in our sample is nearly one third less than the coefficient of variation of P/E (0.60). Nevertheless, since the P/E ratio is so widely known, we will focus on it here.

It is important to stress that firm-specific, country-specific and accounting factors may affect P/E ratios. Thus, we would not expect to see zero variation in P/E ratios across countries any more than we would expect to see zero variation in P/E ratios within a country, even if all firms within a country and across countries employed the same accounting principles. In theory, high-growth companies will have higher P/E ratios than low-growth companies.[4] Since earnings eventually flow through to shareholders as dividends and/or share price appreciation, investors will pay more for an annuity that grows at a faster rate. It is also well known that if interest rates decline in an economy, there will be an increase in P/E ratios for all securities in that country. With lower interest rates, investors place a higher value on future dividends. Thus, we would expect that high growth, low interest rate countries (e.g., Japan) would have higher P/E multiples. In practice, however, investors must form expectations of both future growth and interest rates.

In a series of papers, Paul Aron demonstrates that growth and interest rate variables are not sufficient to explain P/E ratio differences between Japan and the United States.[5] However, once accounting differences (such as methods of depreciation and deferred taxes) are included, Aron suggests that P/E ratios in Japan are in line with those in the United States. Aron's restatement methodology and his overall conclusion have been challenged by Gary Schineman.[6] The alternative view

---

[4]A given change in a firm's growth rate of earnings and dividends will have a larger effect on share price the lower is the firm's cost of capital. See Robert W. Kolb, *Principles of Finance* (Glenview, Ill.: Scott, Foresman, 1988), p. 272.

[5]See Paul Aron, "Japanese P/E Multiples: The Tradition Continues," *Japanese Research Series*, Daiwa Securities America Inc., Report #35, October 23, 1989. Aron's first contribution in this series appeared as Report #24 in 1981.

[6]See Gary Schineman, "Japanese P/E Ratios: Are They Overstated by Conservative Accounting Practices?" *International Research*, Prudential Bache Securities, June 20, 1988; and "Japanese P/E Ratios II: Myth and Reality," *International Research*, Prudential Bache Securities, March 30, 1989.

suggests that Japanese (and other) financial markets have been mispricing securities for some time.[7]

DIVERSITY IN ACCOUNTING, REPORTING, AND AUDITING PRACTICES

Paralleling the diversity in international financial markets are differences that characterize national accounting, reporting, and disclosure practices. Documentation of national differences in accounting measurement systems is provided in Table 4. Examination of this table reveals that most countries subscribe to the consistency, realization, and historical cost principles in preparing their financial statements. Most also value marketable securities and inventory at the lower of cost or market, expense research and development expenditures, offset assets and liabilities when a legal right of offset exists, and exclude minority interest from consolidated income and shareholders' equity. In areas such as the use of discretionary reserves and recording excess depreciation, U.S. practice constitutes minority practice. For most of the measurement rules identified, however, comparative practices among the countries surveyed are mixed. Significant measurement differences between countries relate to multinational consolidations, business combinations, changing prices, deferred taxes, discretionary reserves, foreign currency translation, goodwill, leases, and pensions.

Differences in corporate financial disclosure practices, that is, the communication of accounting measurements to statement readers, constitute another facet of accounting diversity. In an earlier comparative disclosure study, Barrett (1976) concluded that American and British firms exhibited significantly more annual report disclosure than companies from France, Japan, the Netherlands, Sweden, and West Germany. On the other hand, U.S. and U.K. annual reports were not uniformly better than those of the other five countries in terms of specific

---

[7]For more on the pricing of Japanese securities, see also Albert Ando and Alan Auerbach, "The Cost of Capital in the U.S. and Japan: A Comparison," *NBER Working Paper No. 1762*, October 1985; Kenneth French and James Poterba, "Are Japanese Stock Prices Too High?" manuscript, NBER Summer Institute, August 1989; and Jeffrey A. Frankel, "Japanese Finance: A Survey," *NBER Working Paper* No. 3156, November 1989.

categories of information. A subsequent study by Lafferty (1980) including the same countries found great diversity in methods of consolidation, quality of segmental and nonfinancial disclosures, and timeliness of annual report dissemination. In a more recent survey by Choi and Ronen (1988), financial disclosure practices among multinational reporting entities in Asia revealed variation in national disclosure patterns not unlike those found in Europe.

Independent auditors, in reviewing management's financial statement representations, attest to the reliability, fairness, and credibility of those representations. Investors have a big stake in such audits, since their willingness to make decisions increases, and the quality of those decisions should improve when the underlying accounting information is considered reliable. As investors in foreign equities are typically far-removed from the local scene, sensitivity to the attest function is likely to be higher than would otherwise be the case. Differences in national audit practices and procedures add yet another dimension to the notion of accounting diversity.

Table 5 provides some indication of the variation that characterizes the auditor's report. Comparison of audit report elements with those prescribed by an international auditing organization, the International Federation of Accountants, reveals the absence of international harmony in such areas as audit scope, identification of audit standards adhered to, and references to the consistent application of underlying accounting principles.[8] Auditing disparities have also been documented in relation to auditor qualifications, standards of professional independence, audit procedures, and the bases underlying auditing standards.[9]

RESEARCH QUESTION

Our overview of international financial market and accounting characteristics raises the question of whether, and to what extent, variations in the former are associated with variations in the latter. For example,

---

[8]See M. Hussein, "The Auditor's Report: Proposed IFAC Guideline and Current Worldwide Practices," unpublished paper delivered at the annual meeting of the American Accounting Association, San Diego, California, 1982.

[9]See Edward Stamp and Maurice Moonitz, "International Auditing Standards," *CPA Journal*, June 1982, pp. 24, 26, 28–30; July 1982, pp. 48–53.

when financing and investing transactions occur cross-border, do investors require a premium to compensate them for having to deal with unfamiliar accounting practices? Do differences in national accounting requirements cause corporate issuers or listers to avoid certain financial markets in favor of those with less onerous reporting norms? Do accounting differences contribute to capital market inefficiencies in the pricing of corporate securities?

Answers to questions such as these are not intuitively clear. Investors and issuers may be attracted to (or deterred from) certain markets because of institutional reasons (e.g., listing fees, transaction taxes, market liquidity, foreign exchange controls, and so on) unrelated to accounting diversity. We examine next what conventional wisdom has to offer on the linkages between accounting and capital market diversity.

CHAPTER 3

LITERATURE REVIEW: CONVENTIONAL WISDOM ABOUT ACCOUNTING AND CAPITAL MARKETS VERSUS STYLIZED EMPIRICAL FACTS

Little academic research has been devoted to the relationship between accounting diversity and capital markets. However, there is a vast literature on the efficiency of international capital markets and on the subject of accounting information and investor decisions in a general sense. We argue that, indirectly, this existing literature has bearing on our study. For example, if studies of accounting information support the view that accounting measures (generated by numerous accounting systems) provide useful indicators of share price movements, then this suggests that the accounting measures (however generated) provide useful information. This result, however, begs the question of whether some other accounting system would provide still more useful information. If studies of capital market efficiency support the view that market prices reflect available information, then this suggests that markets have been able to correctly decipher the diverse accounting information being presented and set share prices fairly. This result, however, does not address the question of how costly it is for investors to process diverse accounting information, and of whether, based on their analyses, foreign investors are confident enough to participate in international markets to the extent required to hold well-diversified portfolios.

For purposes of presentation, we divide the relevant literature into three categories: (*1*) security pricing and market efficiency, (*2*) accounting diversity and capital market decisions, and (*3*) proposed solutions to the problem of international accounting diversity. In conducting our review, we contrast conventional wisdom on a given subject against related empirical evidence.

SECURITY PRICING AND MARKET EFFICIENCY

In this section, we examine empirical evidence on the efficiency of capital markets outside the United States. We take it as given that U.S. capital markets are highly efficient in the sense that prices fully reflect available information and that consistent, above-average returns are not available.[1]

From the data in Table 1, it is apparent that most European stock markets are considerably smaller than those in the United States, the volume of trading (as a percentage of market capitalization) typically is less, and market capitalization is concentrated in fewer firms. These data could support the conventional notion that European capital markets are more likely to be inefficient in a weak-form sense (i.e., characterized by trends and bandwagons rather than random price movements). To the contrary, the empirical evidence seems to favor, although not conclusively, weak-form efficiency.[2]

In an exhaustive survey of the literature through 1984, Gabriel Hawawini presents a survey of more than 280 studies of European capital markets covering 14 Western European countries. In summarizing the evidence of 112 studies dealing with weak-form efficiency, Hawawini concludes:

> When returns are measured over intervals longer than a week, the Random Walk Model [RWM] cannot be rejected and there is no evidence that mechanical trading rules can be applied to earn abnormal returns net of transaction costs. For subweekly returns the RWM is generally rejected. . . . but these significant deviations from randomness, which are caused

---

[1]For a recent survey of the theoretical and empirical literature on financial market efficiency see Stephen F. LeRoy "Efficient Capital Markets and Martingales," *Journal of Economic Literature* 27 (December 1989), pp. 1583–1621. While most empirical studies are consistent with efficiency, a number of anomalies have emerged which LeRoy concludes "cannot be shrugged off." Some of the anomalies are reviewed in Elroy Dimson, ed., *Stock Market Anomalies* (Cambridge: Cambridge University Press, 1988).

[2]Weak-form efficiency implies that past changes in asset prices are not useful in predicting future price changes in asset prices.

by imperfections in the trading process can not be used by investors to earn abnormal returns.[3]

Table 6 presents a sample of these studies for the French stock market. Notice that the studies by Solnik (1973), Hamon (1975), and Bertoneche (1978) find significant correlation of daily share price changes. While these results may be statistically significant, Hawawini concludes that they are not economically significant in the sense that investors can profit from them.

Our discussion of international accounting principles in Chapter 2 (Table 4) suggested that information disclosure practices in Europe are less revealing than those in the United States. This observation could support a conventional notion that European capital markets are more likely to be semistrong form inefficient (i.e., characterized by slow price adjustment following the release of news).[4] To the contrary, the evidence reviewed by Hawawini seems to favor semistrong-form efficiency.

In summarizing the evidence of 66 studies dealing with semistrong-form efficiency, Hawawini concludes:

> . . . the price adjustment of European shares is generally completed by the time the event has taken place or the specific information has been released. There is little or no post-event price adjustments and no evidence that investors could have consistently earned abnormal . . . returns. The only market that shows some signs of informational inefficiency is the German market. . . . The institutional setting . . . may be partly responsible.[5]

Table 7 presents a sample of these studies of semistrong-form efficiency. Notice that two of the categories in this table deal explicitly with the release of new accounting numbers and changes in accounting rules and reporting methods. The finding that markets quickly reflect the information incorporated in accounting data and that markets are not misled by changes in accounting rules is especially important for us. These

---

[3]Gabriel Hawawini, *European Equity Markets: Price Behavior and Efficiency* (New York University Monograph Series in Finance and Economics, No. 1984–4/5, 1984).

[4]Barrett is one such example. His study of 103 firms and his conclusion that the wide variance between Anglo-American and continental European disclosures could support the belief that continental European equity markets are less efficient than Anglo-American markets. See M. Edgar Barrett, "Financial Reporting Practices: Disclosure and Comprehensiveness in an International Setting," *Journal of Accounting Research*, Spring 1976, pp. 10–26.

[5]Hawawini, *European Equity Markets*, p. 108.

findings suggest that, at the margin, (1) European markets are able to efficiently decipher the accounting information that is provided, and (2) share prices are set that do not leave abnormal returns available for investors armed with public information.

Some investors that we interviewed supported the above view. As one expressed it:

> There often is a big fanfare about so-and-so coming to the U.S. market and having to prepare and release new figures. But we find that when the figures come out, there are very few surprises from what we expected.

Hawawini also reviews the evidence on strong-form tests of market efficiency, that is, whether insiders with access to special information outperform the market. While some studies, such as McDonald (1973) find excess returns, they are often not statistically significant. Hawawini's conclusion regarding strong-form tests is "The evidence surveyed in this section indicates that professionally managed portfolios in Europe do not seem to consistently outperform the market average on a risk-adjusted basis."[6]

A recent study by Cumby and Glen of U.S. mutual funds engaged in international investing supports this general result. The authors find that the professionally managed funds do not outperform naive market indices.[7]

MARKET DIVERSITY, ACCOUNTING INFORMATION, AND INVESTOR DECISIONS

In this section, we review a selection of studies that shed light on how investor decisions are affected by market diversity and accounting information.

The data in Table 1 suggest that the Japanese stock market is the largest in the world, with a market capitalization 25 percent larger than the NYSE. This fact is now conventionally acknowledged, and some institutional investors feel a need to defend their decision to underweight the Japanese market.

---

[6]Ibid. p. 152.

[7]See Robert E. Cumby and Jack D. Glen, "Evaluating the Performance of International Mutual Funds," *Journal of Finance*, June 1990.

One institutional difference between the Japanese and the American stock markets is that cross-holdings in Japan are common (i.e., firm A owning shares of firm B and vice versa), while they are rare in the United States.[8] In a recent paper, French and Poterba demonstrate that cross-holdings have the effect of increasing the market value of listed shares relative to the market value of the productive assets actually owned by the firms.[9] The data in Table 8 reveal that when the figures are adjusted for this cross-holding effect (contrary to the present conventional notion), the market capitalization of the U.S. market *exceeds* that of Japan by about 25 percent. This adjustment reduces the market capitalization weight for Japan from 44.0 percent to 29.5 percent in 1988. The importance of this adjustment for institutional investors who are striving to track the world market is clear. It raises the interesting question of whether institutional investors "saw through" the conventional wisdom when setting their country investment weights.

We now turn to the subject of accounting information and investor decisions. Here the notion that accounting figures are an important source of information to investors and market regulators must certainly be the conventional view among those who decide on accounting principles. Three strands of evidence have emerged in the empirical literature. First are those studies that relate accounting figures with stock market or economic performance. If favorable accounting results are correlated with favorable stock market or economic performance, then this supports the conventional view. The second strand of research examines whether changes in accounting reporting can mislead the market. If change does not mislead the market, then this would suggest that the market also relies on other information when setting share prices, thus diminishing the importance of accounting information. The third strand

---

[8]In other countries, notably Germany, banks are permitted to hold substantial and sometimes controlling interests in non-banking firms. This also leads to the same numerical effect as that which we describe for cross-holdings.

[9]Suppose that Firm A has $100 of net productive assets and 100 shares outstanding, each valued at $1. Suppose that Firm B is similar. Then the market value of these 200 shares of Firms A and B is $200. Now, to introduce a cross-holding effect, let A issue 100 new shares at $1 each that will be held by B as their asset. And let B also issue 100 new shares at $1 each that will be held by A as their asset. Firms A and B now have 400 shares outstanding valued at $400, yet the value of productive physical assets is unchanged. See Kenneth French and James Poterba, "Are Japanese Stock Prices Too High?" manuscript, NBER Summer Institute, August 1989.

considers how capital markets respond to increases in (or deletions from) a standard reporting level. If capital markets respond favorably to an increase in information, then this suggests that accounting information has value and that firms must decide on the optimal amount and type of information to release. We consider these three strands in sequence.

Accounting Information and Stock Prices

Much of the work examining the effects of accounting disclosures on securities prices is predicated on the notion of market efficiency. Loosely defined, market efficiency implies that all information becomes reflected fully in securities prices once it becomes available. Efficiency refers to all information available, including private information; whereas semistrong efficiency refers only to information available publicly. Evidence that a particular item of information is associated, upon its disclosure, with movements in the share price is consistent with the proposition that that item of information has content in the sense of inducing a revision in the investor's assessment of future returns of the security.

In one of the earliest tests of the information content of annual earnings numbers of companies, Ball and Brown used this approach to analyze whether the accounting earnings number is included in the set of relevant information that affects market prices.[10] Specifically, they tested whether foreknowledge of the annual earnings numbers could allow investors to earn abnormal returns. Ball and Brown hypothesized that if the released income number contained new information not already reflected in prices, then good news (actual earnings greater than expected earnings) could cause a firm's stock price to increase, whereas bad news (actual earnings less than expectations) would have the opposite effect. The extent of the association between the income prediction errors and stock price changes was used to indicate the extent to which information contained in the income numbers was used by transactors in the marketplace. The association was observed relative to residual share price changes derived from a market model.

---

[10]See R. Ball and P. Brown, "The Empirical Evaluation of Accounting Income Numbers," *Journal of Accounting Research*, Autumn 1968, pp. 159–77.

The empirical results (summarized in Exhibit 4) were generally in line with Ball and Brown's hypothesis. Stocks with positive prediction errors (good news) tended to outperform the market, and those with negative prediction errors (bad news) tended to do worse than the market. It appears from Exhibit 4 that much of the price change occurred well in advance of the actual release of the income number. Thus, while the accounting numbers seem to have provided investors with information, the results also suggest that investors are following other information sources.

The Ball and Brown study was repeated for a sample of Australian firms and produced similar results (see Exhibit 5). In this case, however, the movement of share prices prior to the announcement date is more erratic than in the United States. This difference may reflect that Australian firms issue semiannual accounting statements, not quarterly ones. It may also reflect institutional differences in the size and trading conditions on the two markets.

Gonedes replicated the Ball and Brown study using a variety of financial ratios in addition to earnings per share to generate measures of market expectations. He found that the earnings per share captured most of whatever information was available from the accounting numbers tested.[11]

Evidence of the importance of business segment disclosures was provided by D. W. Collins. He found that a trading strategy developed from segment-based earnings, not generally available prior to 1970, was profitable.[12] Beaver, Kettler, and Scholes observed a high degree of contemporaneous association between accounting and market risk measures. Specifically, a strategy of ranking and selecting portfolios according to accounting risk measures was found essentially equivalent to a strategy of ranking those same portfolios according to market-determined risk measures. The authors found this to be consistent with hypotheses stating that: (1) accounting data do reflect underlying events that determine differential riskiness among securities and (2) such events are reflected in the market prices of securities.[13]

---

[11]N. Gonedes, "Capital Market Equilibrium and Annual Accounting Numbers: Empirical Evidence," *Journal of Accounting Research*, Spring 1976, pp. 89–137.

[12]D. W. Collins, "SEC Product-Line Reporting and Market Efficiency," *Journal of Financial Economics II*, June 1975, pp. 125–64.

[13]W. Beaver, S. Kettler, and M. Scholes, "The Association between Market Determination and Accounting Determined Risk Measures," *Accounting Review*, October 1970, pp. 654–82.

The Ball and Brown methodology has also been used in numerous related contexts such as quarterly earnings reports (Brown and Kennely, 1972; and Foster, 1978, who used Box-Jenkins expectation models, and non-NYSE stocks). The methodology was also employed by Firth (1976) on the London stock market, Deakin, Norwood, and Smith (1974) on the Tokyo exchange; Ooghe, Beghin, and Verbaere (1981) on Belgian shares; Korhonen (1975) in Finland; Conenberg and Brandi (1976) in West Germany; and Forsgardh and Hertzen (1975) in Sweden.[14] All found statistically significant association between unexpected earnings (defined according to local accounting practices) and unexpected stock returns.

The above evidence supports the conclusion that earnings announcements (current, quarterly, and annual) are associated with changes in the distribution of stock prices. This, in turn, is consistent with the contention that earnings announcements (*including* those generated under U.S. GAAP, U.K. GAAP, Australian GAAP, Swedish GAAP, and so forth) provide timely and relevant information to the marketplace.

Changes in Accounting Rules

Another strand of research has tested the hypothesis that capital markets are not misled by accounting rule changes. If this hypothesis cannot be rejected, it would support the conventional notion (among academic researchers) that the selection of accounting rules need not pose a barrier, because the market uses other channels to uncover the true economic condition of firms.

In a study of 197 firms making 247 accounting rule changes (including changes in depreciation policy, inventory methods, consolidation policy, accounting for investments and revenue recognition between 1947 and 1961, Ball concluded that the markets were not fooled.[15] Based on Exhibit 6, it appears that the firms that adopted accounting rule changes tended to display a pattern of lower returns relative to the market. The results suggest that these firms may have adopted accounting changes to improve the appearance of their reported accounting

---

[14]See the Bibliography at the back of the book for full citations.

[15]R. Ball, "Changes in Accounting Techniques and Stock Prices," *Empirical Research in Accounting, Selected Studies, 1972* (supplement), *Journal of Accounting Research* 10 (Spring 1972), pp. 1–38.

numbers. Capital markets apparently saw through these decisions, since share prices moved well in advance of the accounting changes.

In another study related to accounting rule changes, Choi et al. analyze a sample of Japanese and Korean financial statements transformed into U.S. GAAP.[16] The authors find substantial differences between the financial ratios of the selected companies and a matching sample of U.S. firms. The authors conclude that a variety of country specific factors (e.g., institutional, cultural, political and tax considerations) are associated with the difference between their financial ratios and U.S. norms. As a result, the authors conclude that the restated Japanese and Korean ratios are meaningless when considered in isolation. Extracting information from the numbers depends on an understanding of the environmental and economic context. This is strong evidence that simple restatement may not be sufficient to achieve useful information and international comparability.

In a related study on restatement, Choi and Hong examine the usefulness of restating accounting data from one set of accounting principles to another.[17] The authors test the decision utility of restated numbers by applying a ranking measure to restated and unrestated accounting-based financial ratios. Choi and Hong find no significant change in enterprise rankings after restatement. In order to test the predictive value of adjusted data, the authors measure the correlation of restated data with market returns in the subsequent year. The correlation is negligible, suggesting that restated accounting information possesses little decision utility. The findings, although limited because of data constraints, suggest that the market is making wide use of available information, beyond the information that is contained in reported numbers.

Changes in the Level of Reporting

While obvious rule changes or simple restatements of accounting numbers may have no information value, the third strand of empirical litera-

---

[16]Frederick D. S. Choi et al., "Analyzing Foreign Financial Statements: The Use and Misuse of International Ratio Analysis," *Journal of Business Studies*, Spring/Summer 1983, pp. 113–31.

[17]Frederick D. S. Choi and S. B. Hong, "The Decision Utility of Restating Accounting Information Sets: Korea," *Advances in Financial Planning and Forecasting*, ed. Raj Aggarwal, Greenwich, Conn.: JAI Press, forthcoming).

ture considers how capital markets respond to increases in (or deletions from) a standard level of accounting reporting. The notion that capital markets might respond favorably to an increase in information follows from the standard principal–agent problem in the context of asymmetric information.[18] In this traditional corporate finance problem, the presumption is that entrepreneurs know all of the economic attributes of their risky enterprises. In order to raise capital at economic rates, they must reveal enough about the firm to shareholders and bondholders. These stakeholders are risk averse, and they will reward the entrepreneur with lower required rates of return as they receive more information that lowers the perceived risk of the project. But the entrepreneur cannot reveal too much, in part because it is costly to provide this information and, in addition, because competitors may be encouraged to enter the market. In this context, the entrepreneur must choose the optimal amount and type of information to release.

Choi has adapted this argument to the case of firms operating in global capital markets. He describes the case for more standardized and complete disclosure as follows:

> Increased firm disclosure tends to improve the subjective probability distributions of a security's expected return streams in the mind of an individual investor by reducing the uncertainty associated with the return stream. For firms which generally outperform the industry average, it is also argued that improved financial disclosure will tend to increase the relative weighting which an investor will place on favorable firm statistics relative to other information vectors which he utilizes in making judgments with respect to the firm. Both of the foregoing effects will entice an individual to pay a larger amount for a given security than otherwise, thus lowering a firm's cost of capital.[19]

---

[18]The principal-agent literature considers how one individual (a principal) can design a compensation system (a contract) that establishes incentives for another individual (the agent) to behave in the principal's interests. The principal-agent relationship is defined by implicit and/or explicit contracts which gives rise to the costs of structuring, monitoring and enforcing such contracts. The nature of these agency costs, the incentives for entrepreneurs to release information and for investors to procure information are discussed in Jensen and Meckling (1973). See also Ross (1973) and Jensen (1983).

[19]Frederick D. S. Choi, "Financial Disclosure in Relation to a Firm's Capital Costs," *Accounting and Business Research*, Autumn 1973a, pp. 282–92.

The hypothesis that a firm would tailor its provision of accounting information to achieve a financial objective can be subjected to empirical testing. In a study of European firms, mostly multinationals, that were preparing to issue bonds on the Eurobond market, Choi concluded that the majority of firms preceded their offering by an increase in the volume and quality of their financial disclosures.[20] The results suggest that these actions were taken to lower the cost of funds and increase the chances for a successful offering. And during the study period, the Eurobond market was indeed the low cost source for corporate funding.

A recent study by Meek and Gray reaches much the same conclusion, but in the context of the equity market.[21] Meek and Gray examine 28 continental European firms with shares listed on the London Stock Exchange. The authors find that the companies have exceeded Exchange requirements through a wide range of voluntary disclosures. In some cases, the authors conclude, the additional voluntary disclosures were "substantial." These results suggest that firms have found it in their interest to provide additional accounting disclosures in the hope of improving their share prices, reducing their cost of funds, and competing with other firms for capital in the international market. In addition, Meek and Gray report that firms display national patterns in what they choose to disclose and not disclose. The authors highlight "forecast information in Sweden, changing price information in The Netherlands, employee disclosures in France and social reporting in Germany" as particular areas of concern to firms.

SOLUTIONS TO THE PROBLEM OF ACCOUNTING DIVERSITY

As we argued in Chapter 1, the case for harmonization of international accounting principles is often taken as irrefutable. The conventional wisdom in this category might be two-fold. First, active public policy

---

[20]Frederick D. S. Choi, "Financial Disclosure and Entry to the European Capital Market," *Journal of Accounting Research*, Autumn 1973b, pp. 159–75.

[21]G. K. Meek and S. J. Gray, "Globalization of Stock Markets and Foreign Listing Requirements: Voluntary Disclosures by Continental European Companies Listed on the London Stock Exchange," *Journal of International Business Studies* 20, no. 2 (Summer 1989), pp. 315–36.

initiatives are desirable to set standards regarding international accounting principles and financial disclosure. Second, harmonization of international accounting principles and financial disclosure is a necessary part of developing a large, well-functioning international financial market. There is empirical evidence, however, that contradicts both of these conventional notions, despite their intuitive appeal.

A study by Benston examines the efficacy of private regulatory, or self-regulatory, bodies in the United Kingdom.[22] He concludes that private regulatory agencies have successfully balanced the needs of their constituencies (listed companies and financial firms) with the public's interest. In that respect, this source for financial regulation has been as effective as a public body, such as the SEC.

In the study by Choi discussed above, it is clear that the development of the Eurobond market into a world-class market was not impeded by the lack of strict rules for issuers on accounting principles and disclosure. Firms from around the world were able to enter this market and respond to competitive pressures, trading off the costs of producing and disclosing information with the demands for information by investors.

These results, in general, are illustrative of what has been called the regulatory dialectic.[23] In an international setting with many regulatory bodies, competition will determine the equilibrium level of regulation affecting different financial firms. In the cases we have reviewed, if a financial market requires too much accounting information or regulatory burdens, firms will migrate to another region. The development of the Euromarkets as a response to excessive domestic financial market regulation is an important example of this behavior.[24] On the other hand, if a financial market requires too little accounting information or regulatory guidance, private firms will find it in their interests to supply more.

---

[22]George J. Benston, "Public (U.S.) Compared to Private (U.K.) Regulation of Corporate Financial Disclosure," *Accounting Review*, July 1976, pp. 483–98.

[23]See Edward J. Kane, "Competitive Financial Reregulation: An International Perspective," in *Threats to International Financial Stability*, ed. R. Portes and A. Swoboda (London: Cambridge University Press, 1987).

[24]See Gunter Dufey, *The Eurobond Market: Function and Future* (Seattle: University of Washington Graduate School of Business), 1969; and Richard M. Levich, "The Euromarkets after 1992," in *European Banking after 1992*, ed. Jean Dermine (London: Basil Blackwood 1990).

The research findings of Benston (1976), Choi (1973b), and Meek and Gray (1989) illustrate this type of private, voluntary behavior.

Overall, these findings cast doubt on the wisdom of applying too tight a grip on requirements pertaining to accounting principles, accounting disclosures, or other regulatory actions. If accounting principles are designed to reflect environmental norms, then accounting principles will be identical only where the underlying economics are identical. The actions of the Bank for International Settlements to harmonize international banking regulations may set the stage for harmonization of accounting rules in that industry. Without a similar harmonization of fundamental economic incentives and regulation in the broad range of other international industries, the case for harmonization of international accounting principles and disclosure practices remains an empirical issue.

SUMMARY

In this chapter, we have reviewed empirical evidence on financial market efficiency and market responses to accounting information. The evidence seems to suggest that capital markets outside the United States are functioning efficiently and able to cope with diverse accounting regimes and institutional arrangements. A cursory look at the evidence (see Table 9) suggests a huge growth in international stock transactions over the 1982–1988 period.[25] Notwithstanding this rosy appraisal of international capital markets, our survey begs two questions that are of concern to policy makers. First, would a common, harmonized accounting system provide more useful information to market participants than the diverse systems now in place? Second, even though financial markets may appear efficient, do diverse accounting systems act as a nontariff barrier, affecting the capital market decisions of investors and issuers? The results of our survey address these two questions.

---

[25]See also Michael Howell and Angela Cozzini, *International Equity Flows: 1989 Edition* (London: Salomon Brothers, 1989).

CHAPTER 4

RESEARCH METHODOLOGY, SURVEY DESIGN, AND DATA PREPARATION

An ultimate objective for research in the area of international accounting and capital markets would be to determine quantitatively the impact of international accounting diversity on the prices of securities and on the volume and location of trading in these securities. Obviously, securities pricing and the location and growth of market activity are complex processes affected by numerous macroeconomic and institutional factors.

In Exhibit 1, we illustrated the wide variation in price-to-earnings ratios that we observe across countries. There are many economic reasons why price-to-earnings ratios, price-to-cash-flow ratios, and other financial statistics may differ across national markets. To repeat only two of the possible reasons, differential national interest rates could cause identical expected earnings or cash flow streams to be capitalized at different discount rates. Cross-holding of corporate shares among related parties in one market could restrict the supply of tradable shares leading to a positive bias in share prices in that market. The key question for this study is to what extent might such ratio differences be due to national accounting differences; that is, to what extent might accounting differences affect the "E" in the P/E comparison?

Similarly, we observe that investors from different countries differ considerably as to whether they hold broadly or narrowly diversified international stock portfolios. Howell and Cozzini report that international holdings of U.K. investors are three times as great as those of U.S. investors.[1] We also observe (Table 1) that foreign firms tend to

---

[1] Michael Howell and Angela Cozzini, *International Equity Flows: 1989 Edition* (London: Salomon Brothers, 1989).

concentrate their issuing or listing activity in certain markets rather than others. Again, these investor and issuer decisions are determined in complex ways. But our key concern is, to what extent might variations in national accounting and reporting practices contribute to the patterns that we observe? Would permissive accounting rules in one country cause investors to favor shares of companies whose accounting standards are less flexible? Do differential disclosure requirements bias corporate issuing or listing decisions toward or away from certain capital markets?

As an empirical matter, in the absence of a well-specified model of the equilibrium pricing of securities in various national markets, it is impossible to conclude whether security prices have been or are misaligned. It is also impossible to ascertain whether international capital flows and portfolio holdings of securities have been suboptimal.

Much of the empirical evidence that we reviewed in Chapter 3 seems to support the notion that non-U.S. security markets function fairly efficiently. This conclusion seems to hold even without adjusting for economic considerations, such as differential size, which might also affect market efficiency. However, without a benchmark representing the fair pricing of securities or the ideal holdings in international portfolios, it is impossible to determine analytically whether international accounting diversity is inhibiting agents from hitting their benchmark targets.

As a result, our objectives in this phase of the research must be less ambitious than our ultimate aim of providing quantitative measures of the impact of accounting diversity on prices and market preferences. Our approach is to gather information directly from capital market participants using a structured but open-ended interview format. Our hope is that these discussions will clarify the nature and scope of the problems associated with accounting differences and thereby suggest a set of specific quantifiable relationships that will provide the basis for future research.

The goals of this study, diagrammed in Exhibit 7, are to survey a cross-section of users and providers of international accounting statements to ascertain which groups experience problems when dealing with international accounting diversity and to have them describe the nature of these problems. We will also assess how users and preparers cope with accounting diversity and whether their coping mechanisms are successful. If coping is not successful, we attempt to ascertain whether or not there is an associated perceived capital market effect. If the participants in our sample are representative of the broader population, our findings will suggest whether there is a capital market effect from international accounting diversity. A discussion of plausible solutions will then be in order.

SAMPLE DESIGN

In order to arrive at a representative sample for our survey interviews, we stratified the universe of accounting statement readers and preparers into several dimensions—geographic location, user group, and size. Our reasoning for this stratification is as follows.

To be sure that the information we gathered had a direct bearing on our research questions, we sampled participants domiciled in countries whose accounting and reporting practices depart quite significantly from international norms, that is, those of the United States and United Kingdom—hence, the decision to query statement users in Japan, West Germany, and Switzerland. We also wanted to include financial markets whose investment institutions have a significant stake in foreign securities and which are active in trading. In the interest of time and resources, we narrowed our choice to Frankfurt, London, New York, Tokyo, and Zurich.

We identified institutional investors, corporate issuers, investment underwriters, and market regulators as the primary audience of interest for international accounting statements. To uncover issues that might not be captured by interviewing direct users of or preparers of accounting information, we also interviewed representatives of ratings agencies, an international financial data service, and an organization working towards international accounting harmony. Individuals queried had to be high enough in the management hierarchy to have decision responsibility, that is, actually make international investment, funding, underwriting, and regulatory decisions. And, as organizational size may affect the degree of sophistication that is brought to bear on dealing with international accounting differences, we decided to interview representatives of both large and less large organizations.

Reasoning that accounting differences would have a greater impact on the valuation of international equity as opposed to debt securities, we focused more attention on equity investments, equity issues, and listings as opposed to bonds.

Our focus on equity issues reflects a compromise. As one of our interviewees would remark:

To buy the bonds of a foreign company, all you really need to know is its rating. To make a portfolio investment, you need better information to gauge the firm's prospects but not absolute precision. But if you're buying the *entire* company, then you really need high quality information—to see through the accounting statements into the real value of the firm.

While merger and acquisition (M&A) activity may require the most sophisticated understanding of foreign accounting practices and, therefore, have the greatest chance of uncovering the possible difficulties raised by accounting diversity, there are several problems. First, M&A activity is relatively recent. The volume of transactions is relatively small in comparison to international portfolio flows.[2] Second, M&A activity is often transaction specific and personality specific. This lowers the chance that a large sample of the key players could be identified. Finally, M&A transactions often involve privileged information. We felt that it was highly unlikely that individuals would share sensitive information of this sort. For these reasons, we decided to survey the larger universe of equity portfolio managers.[3]

This sample design produced a total of 52 institutions, distributed across various categories as shown in Exhibit 8. The names of these institutions are listed in Appendix 1. Because of the expense associated with the survey method (especially in an international context), our sample is not large. However, survey respondents were selected in largely random fashion, and, hence, our findings should be fairly representative.

SURVEY METHODOLOGY

As our primary focus is on respondent attitudes, behavior, and reasons behind such, we used personal interviews as our method of gathering

---

[2]Estimates of the size of international M&A activity vary. Walter and Smith (1989, p. 44) report that between 1982 and 1988, over 3,400 deals involving at least one non-U.S. counterparty were completed with a value of nearly $500 billion. In 1988, Walter and Smith estimate 847 such deals with a value of $120 billion. Howell and Cozzini (1989, p. 20) estimate that many more international M&A deals took place in 1988 (around 2,500) but with a similar value of $124.8 billion. This value is small relative to total secondary market turnover in international equities, which Howell and Cozzini estimate as $1,212 billion. However, international M&A activity appears large relative to the flow of net new money placed in international equities, which Howell and Cozzini place at $21.1 billion in 1988.

[3]Several people did refuse to grant interviews, one claiming that he did not want to reveal privileged information about how he analyzes international stocks.

data. To assist in this effort, we constructed a questionnaire that included factual and behavioral questions relating to decision processes, information requirements, nature of accounting diversity, coping mechanisms, and capital market effects. In addition to responses of the yes/no variety, most questions were left open-ended to enable us to learn more about why a particular response was given and the nature of such a response. The questionnaire was pretested in New York, including circulation among academic colleagues specializing in accounting, finance, economics, and behavioral science. A sample of the interview questionnaire used for the "Investor" category is included in Appendix 2.

The interviews ranged from one to four hours in length, averaging about two hours. Nearly all of the interviews were conducted by two individuals to minimize bias and misinterpretation of responses. A language translator accompanied the interviewers in those instances where the interview subject requested one. All interview subjects were sent a sample of the interview questions in advance, and some institutions prepared written answers ahead of time. All interview subjects were promised that their remarks would be kept confidential. We used a tape recorder during each interview and prepared a written transcript.

To condense the information contained in these often wide-ranging discussions, we prepared a second form, coding 23 key items from each interview. These 23 items are listed in Table 10. Some of these 23 items are objective, descriptive items that are fairly easily coded. Other items presented more difficulty.

The question that is of primary interest here is No. 13, "Does accounting diversity affect your capital market decisions?" Some interview subjects gave unequivocal answers to this question. Others did not. For example, a subject might have said, "I am troubled by German accounting, but not British," or "I am troubled with insurance companies, but not manufacturing firms," or "I *was* troubled by accounting diversity, but not any longer." In some decentralized institutions, we found conflicting views among individuals interviewed in sequence. And most troublesome for us was the response by one institution:

> The official answer of this institution to your question is "No;" accounting diversity is not a problem for us. But personally, I feel that it is a problem.

To the best of our abilities, we coded answers that were most representative of the opinions we heard expressed and the actions we observed taken by the institution.

CHAPTER 5

SURVEY FINDINGS

In this chapter we present the main findings of our interviews with representatives of the 52 institutions in our sample. Our primary focus is the key question: Does accounting diversity affect your capital market decisions? We begin with an overview of the results for the entire sample, with cross-tabulations across the major strata. We then analyze the results for the primary categories in our sample—investors, issuers, underwriters, regulators, and others. Within each category, we describe some of the related findings from our questionnaire, for example, how the respondents define accounting diversity, which countries they feel are the most troublesome in terms of regulations or accounting principles, which accounting items are the most troublesome, and so forth. Most of our attention, however, is on examining the patterns that we find across the "Yes" and "No" respondents to our key question and documenting the coping mechanisms that they employ.

OVERVIEW OF THE FINDINGS

A summary of the answers to the question of whether international accounting diversity affects capital market decisions is in Table 11. Of the 52 institutions we surveyed, one was actually an agency charged with promoting accounting harmony. We omitted this institution as it was not itself a preparer or direct user of accounting statements and did not make capital market decisions itself. Of the 51 remaining institutions, the responses were evenly split, 24 "Yes," 26 "No," and one institution unable to clearly answer the question. Both the investor group and the issuer group were fairly evenly split, with a majority of investors (9 of 17) responding that accounting diversity did affect capital market decisions, while a majority of issuers (9 of 15) responded that it did not.

Nearly all of the underwriters in our sample (7 of 8) felt that accounting diversity affected their capital market decisions. We believe this stems from the function of underwriters as intermediaries who deal with numerous issuers and investors. At the other extreme, *all* of the regulatory institutions in our sample (8 of 8) responded that accounting diversity did *not* affect their capital market decisions. We believe that it is appropriate to address our key question to regulators, since most non-U.S. regulators analyze original source financial statements and could be affected by accounting diversity. Note that our key question does not ask whether *regulatory* diversity affects the capital markets that regulators regulate, which is a separate topic we take up in our discussion of regulators.

Based on these results, 48 percent of those responding claim that accounting diversity affects their capital market decisions, and we must reject the hypothesis that there is no affect. In addition, the summary results also show that underwriters and regulators stand out as different from the average of the whole sample.

We then cross-tabulated the results using five descriptive categories—country, size, experience, scope of activity, and organizational structure. The results are shown in Table 12. For each cross-tabulation, we constructed a chi-square statistic to test for independence of "Yes" and "No" responses within each category. In each case, we could not reject the hypothesis that the "Yes" and "No" responses split proportionately, regardless of country, size, experience, scope, or organizational structure.[1] Understandably, we found significant positive correlation among the size, experience, and scope of activity measures.

INSTITUTIONAL INVESTOR RESPONSES

Cross-border security investments have been spurred by a number of developments. These developments include (1) advances in telecommunications technology, (2) increased awareness of opportunities for enhanced portfolio returns and risk reduction through international diversification, (3) gradual deregulation of national capital markets, (4) removal of foreign exchange and capital controls in many countries, (5)

---

[1]We decided that "size" was not a relevant category for regulators and they were excluded from the calculation, resulting in a 24 and 17 split.

development of the Eurocurrency markets, and (6) greater access to financial information.[2]

The growth in foreign purchases and sales of U.S. stocks and, conversely, U.S. purchases and sales of foreign equities by various countries was discussed in conjunction with Table 9. As institutional investors account for much of this volume, we queried portfolio managers of major investment companies who had responsibility for making cross-country investment choices. We now review the principal findings for this user group.

Information Requirements and Accounting Diversity

In making their investment choices, investment managers rely on several types of data. These information types include market parameters, macroeconomic data, political intelligence, regulatory considerations, differential taxes, and firm-specific information. While macroeconomic data and information on market parameters influence asset allocation decisions and country weightings, firm-specific information is used in facilitating specific stock selections. This suggests that accounting information is one of several necessary components of an institutional investor's information set. In the words of one investor:

> In making our global asset allocations, accounting practices are at the moment not so important. But when we come down to another level, when we have an exposure to the British equities market or say the Japanese bond market, and we have to pick up stocks or bonds to build a portfolio, then accounting differences are important.

To quote another investor:

> Knowledge of national accounting and reporting practices is of major importance in determining national asset classes (at its simplest, a national portfolio) based on forecasts. As we have already dealt with the allocation of the individual asset categories in our investment strategy, "all" that is necessary for the choice/grouping within the asset classes is a knowledge of national accounting and reporting regulations. The lack of standardization in these regulations presents an insurmountable barrier

---

[2]See the report of the U.S. Government Accounting Office, *International Finance: Regulation of International Securities Markets* (Washington, D.C.: GAO, 1989).

(for the time being, at least) to comparisons between asset categories. Clearly, the way of solving this problem that would provide by far the greatest advantages would be by managing special funds, for example, a fund for insurance stocks around the world. To add a qualifying point here, however, all empirical examinations undertaken to date have not been able to substantiate conclusively the existence of a globally valid "industry factor."

At each interview, we asked each subject to define the term *accounting diversity*. To nearly every investor, accounting diversity connotes differences in accounting principles.

> Whenever I look at U.S. annual reports, I wish there were no differences in accounting. For example, Japanese companies value their marketable securities at cost whereas U.S. companies value them at market. It's very difficult for our analysts to compare a domestic with an American company.[3]

To most investors, accounting diversity also refers to differences in corporate financial disclosure practices. And some investors associate the term with differences in national audit practices.

Countries, Industries, and Accounting Items of Concern

Countries or regions whose accounting principles were mentioned as a source of concern for analysts when investing outside the home country are, in alphabetical order, Australia, continental Europe, France, Hong Kong, Japan, Korea, Latin America, Luxembourg, Norway, Portugal, Switzerland, the United States, and West Germany. Of this set, countries most frequently mentioned were Japan, Switzerland, West Germany, and the United States. In the words of one investor:

> Comparisons are more feasible for a U.S. company, a U.K. company, or an Australian company. Scandinavia is improving. The Japanese companies are a nightmare. In Europe, even within countries, there may be significant differences in reporting. As a general rule, in Europe, the closer you get to Switzerland, the worse the financial reporting becomes. I think when analysts try to compare companies to better understand the

---

[3]Actually, U.S. generally accepted accounting principles require that companies account for marketable securities at the lower of cost or market.

prospects of a company they are limited. It is virtually impossible to compare a company in one country with one in another country.

Industries identified as posing analysts with similar difficulties include banking, insurance, financial services in general, semiconductors, and mining. Differences in generally accepted accounting principles (GAAP) that prove troublesome to those interviewed include a whole array of measurement rules. Accounting principles most frequently mentioned relate to multinational consolidations, valuation of fixed assets, deferred taxes, pensions, marketable securities, discretionary reserves, foreign currency transactions and translation, leases, goodwill, depreciation, long-term construction contracts, inventory valuation, and provisions.

Similar country and industry responses were noted with respect to financial disclosure differences. Half of the respondents reported being hindered by the absence of comparable disclosure standards. Disclosure items most frequently mentioned were segmental information, methods of asset valuation, foreign operations disclosures, frequency and completeness of interim information, description of capital expenditures, hidden reserves, and off-balance sheet-items.

The absence of comparable standards of disclosure are not always viewed as a hindrance, however. In the opinion of one investor:

> Sometimes the lack of disclosure provides you with investment opportunities. The point is, if you do a big effort, not on the accounts, because it is not transparent anyway, but in understanding the company, then maybe you can make a lot of money. This is because your competitors, that is, the other players in the market, may not have devoted the right amount of analysis to a particular company as you have. I am not referring to the use of inside information!

Accounting Diversity and Investor Decisions

Out of the 17 investors we interviewed, nine replied that differences in national accounting principles hindered the measurement of their decision variables and ultimately affected their investment decisions. Examples of what they meant by their responses can be seen from the following quotes:[4]

---

[4] Quotes from different individuals that appear in a series are labeled (A), (B), and so forth.

Comparisons of reported performance between Japanese and non-Japanese companies are made more difficult by differences in accounting treatment. For example, many Korean companies are using straight-line depreciation, while the majority of Japanese companies employ the declining method. While cash flow analysis can provide you with some answers, in order for us to give an accurate picture of the companies in each country, some adjustments must be made for accounting differences. While this is easy to say, it is difficult to implement. (A)

If you are given an earnings figure in the United States, I think you can assume that the figure is correct. Of course, the earnings number may differ depending on the principles of accounting employed, such as different methods of inventory costing. But, you can generally say that the reported earnings figures are correct. If you look at the earnings figures in Switzerland, these figures may not be correct. In Switzerland, dividends are not adapted to reported earnings; rather, earnings are adapted to dividends. Since most Swiss companies maintain stable dividend payments, reported earnings are tied to dividend patterns and not the other way around. By building up hidden assets, or by diminishing them, companies can manage reported earnings. There are companies that publish good earnings figures, but most Swiss companies' published earnings figures are not correct. So for the analyst, it's very difficult. He has to estimate the real earnings, not only in the future, but also the actual and past earnings. (B)

However, the seven investors in our sample that did not feel hindered by accounting differences supplied us with a different image, as the following responses indicate.

We don't spend a lot of time getting hung up on accounting differences in most sectors, because it's not really appropriate in many cases to bring the standards back to U.S. GAAP. If the major market is driven by the Germans, or the English, or whoever, it's more important to understand the books they're looking at and the motivation behind the ways they are constructed. (A)

We devote a lot of time to what I call the economic analysis of the company. That is, we analyze the company's business, sectors of activity, whether they have a new product, where the competition is, are the margins going up or down, are they losing market share, increasing market share, do they have legal problems, that sort of thing. Plus, one thing—we believe that companies are run by people, and we try to meet them. So we make company calls and we try to, sort of, *feel* the company. But the financial side of the aspects of our analysis—well, I'm not saying we don't do it. It's one part of our analysis, but only one part of it, and not the essential part of it. (B)

It is difficult for us to make a complete analysis of a foreign company's financial position. Although we carry out as much research as possible, we believe it is more practical to use financial information provided by local brokers and research institutes. As we do not directly analyze the financial position of foreign companies, and as we adopt a top-down investment approach, we are not affected by differences in accounting methods, and we are not doing anything in particular to cope with this diversity. If we attempted to do so, it would probably be very costly. (C)

We examined the correlation between these responses and various characteristics of the investor's institution. Our analysis revealed no apparent correlation of investor responses with either investor size, country-of-domicile, organizational structure, length of experience in international investing, scope of international investments, or investment approach.

Our analysis of the interview responses suggests that problems posed by accounting diversity may also be a function of the coping mechanisms adopted by users for dealing with diversity. We now review those coping mechanisms and examine if any patterns are apparent.

Investor Coping Mechanisms

For those investors responding that accounting diversity is not a problem that affects their capital market decisions, four coped by developing a multiple principles capability (MPC), that is, undertaking to familiarize themselves with foreign accounting principles and adopt a local perspective when analyzing foreign financial statements.

You cannot compare very easily across markets. You can't use the same stock picking, the same valuation techniques. The kind of political risks you see in Hong Kong, you don't see in West Germany and vice versa. In almost every single market in the world, local investors predominate, and local investors control the valuation system. These local investors are parochial beings and they don't necessarily know or care how valuation systems work elsewhere in the world. They have their own way, and they've been doing it this way for quite a long time. As a foreigner sometimes you can come in with a different way of looking at things and spot a kind of value that the locals haven't spotted, but it's pretty rare. And, betting against the local investment community in a major way, saying, "you guys have just got this market completely wrong" is unlikely usually to make you a whole lot of money.

Another coped in the following manner:

> One way to deal with accounting differences is to compare the rate of change of a company's performance over time. While accounting differences are important, it is not so much of a problem to us at this time. It is true, however, that we must be aware of differences in regulatory accounting requirements.

In lieu of coping in an accounting sense, three investors coped by relying on information variables less sensitive to corporate accounting treatment. Specifically, one institutional investor uses a dividend discount model as opposed to a discounted earnings framework as a basis for its investment decisions. To quote that individual:

> The attraction of using a dividend-driven, rather than an earnings-driven, valuation framework is that dividends, as hard cash paid to shareholders, are supposedly more free of definitional differences than other variables. In addition, there are differences in the timing of company reports relative to year ends. . . . This is not to say that dividend data is entirely free from distortion. Our valuation framework takes explicit account of timing differences. And issues of taxation, corporate culture, and corporate financing can have important implications for the differences in the level of payout and the attraction of dividends between different markets. In our view, the economic rationale behind these differences is an important component of our research. In general, since the asset allocation decision is the most crucial in determining relative investment performance, we believe we can benefit more, and a great deal, from the investigation of implications of these issues on growth, its financing and valuation than from an attempt to rebase national earnings data, for example, to a single standard. The costs of such investigations are, of course, substantial, in terms of research resources.

Another investor copes successfully with accounting diversity by relying solely on macroeconomic variables in making asset allocations by country and then investing in a diversified portfolio of securities within each country. Finally, one investor circumvents the problem of accounting differences by relying primarily on sociological trends in making investment picks. This involves first seeing in what direction consumer preferences are moving and then investing in industry leaders that are expected to capitalize on such trends.

The nine investors whose decisions were affected by accounting diversity also coped in various ways. Seven investors dealt with diverse accounting principles by restating from one set of measurement rules to a framework more familiar to the user. In five of the seven cases, restatements were made informally by mentally adjusting for major differences in accounting measurements. The following quote is illustrative of the informal style:

> We cope by trying to figure out what the local reported numbers might mean from a U.S. perspective. In general, we don't really restate the foreign financial statements formally. In going through the annual report, we'll make an adjustment right in the annual report and write it down. I am aware of one effort to attempt to formally restate from one set of accounting standards to another. But in my opinion the task is really too big for someone to competently handle it.

Two investors engaged in a more formal restatement process.

> In doing my investment analyses, I try to understand the real earnings and real net worth of a company. So I restate the reported numbers to a U.S. GAAP basis. (A)

> We adopt a two-stage approach to our analysis. We first restate the foreign financial statements to our country's GAAP to enable us to better understand the company. Then we compare that company with companies in the local market to see if it's a good buy. (B)

Coping with accounting diversity was also accomplished by adopting different investment strategies. One large investor chose, for the moment at least, to limit its exposure to foreign equities, concentrating instead on government or quasi-government investments, for example, bonds. Investments in equities have been limited to countries whose accounting principles are not very different from their own. At the time of our visitation, however, this particular organization was in the midst of forming a separate department to specifically deal with international equity investments and accounting differences.

Another institutional investor copes by adopting a top-down approach to foreign investments. According to the representatives interviewed:

> So far we don't attempt to compare results between countries. This does not mean that we do not want to do it. But thus far, we do not have the

capability to do it. We have tried it in the past and have had disappointing results. . . . I think that if the investor could be convinced that there is more reliable information available, he would take a more active approach and rely on individual companies. At present, this is not the case and may be why so many investors have taken a passive approach and just invest in the index. Such a development would allow analysts to come up with more reasonable forecasts. . . . Within a country, if no reliable information is provided, then we stick to the well-known companies in that country and do not consider the second- or third-tier companies.

Capital Market Effects

For the nine investors whose decisions were affected by accounting differences, such diversity did result in capital market effects. These effects, reported separately for GAAP differences and disclosure differences, are summarized in Table 13.

As can be seen, accounting differences were deemed to have significant capital market effects. These effects relate to the location of market activity, the types of companies invested in, and pricing of international securities. Because of the size of the institutions we surveyed, information processing costs associated with accounting differences were generally not considered significant. However, this was not the case for all investors.

The following testimonials provide some insight into the ways in which capital market effects are manifested.

> Accounting differences which affect the "E" in the P/E ratio partly explain why we are underweighted in Japan. (A)
>
> We have thus far restricted our target investments to governmental investments, that is, investment in government bonds has reduced the need for us to concern ourselves with the accounting diversity issue. However, when we move to corporate stock investments in foreign countries, the accounting diversity problem will be of concern to us, and we will have to address it. (B)
>
> Differences in accounting principles make it difficult for us to interpret the ratings assigned to companies. If the differences cannot be verified, we place less credibility on the ratings. (C)
>
> We don't care if accounting differences are great if you can buy the foreign stock at a cheap enough price. (D)
>
> We expect to earn a higher break-even return on firms whose accounting results make them appear to be more risky.(E)

The impact of national differences in the accounting treatment of purchased goodwill has given U.K. companies an advantage over U.S. companies in bidding for merger candidates. (F)

Investors were evenly divided on the question of whether their decisions are affected by differences in financial disclosure practices. For the "No" group, coping generally took the form of company visitations to secure added information. One investor explained the benefits of this approach as follows:

> We make a great effort to go and talk to companies, because the mentality in my country is, "I don't put that in my annual report because my competition will see it." Companies will tell you a lot of things in person, but there are exceptions. The information obtained comes off so much better across somebody's desk, because they know we're not going to publish a report, they know we're not the press, we're not the competition, so they're very friendly with information once you develop a relationship of trust and confidence with them.

Coping with differential disclosures sometimes takes the form of assigning firms into investment versus speculative grades. Firms providing full disclosure are classified into the former category, while firms that are less forthcoming are put into the latter.

Investors who say that disclosure differences affect their investment decisions generally cope in similar fashion as the "no effect" group. Corporate visitations are a frequently mentioned coping mechanism. "Financial coping" is also practiced. To wit:

> If we have enough information about the company, we engage in active individual stock selection. If we do not, then we take a passive approach and adopt a mutual fund approach. For example, if a Thai company does not provide sufficient information, we will not include such stock on our "master list" of approved stocks to purchase. However, we might invest in a Thai mutual fund if the macro considerations are also favorable.

Decision problems caused by financial disclosure differences are associated with capital market effects. The effects, reported in Table 13 are not unlike those associated with GAAP differences.

One investor describes the link between differential corporate financial disclosure and market effects in this manner:

> Share prices in the local market tend to be affected by local investors. Therefore, as long as local investors accept local disclosure practices,

local share prices will not be affected one way or the other by disclosure differences. But, it does make a difference to the international portfolio manager. He will be fairly nervous about a company that has limited disclosure. Consequently, their interest in those companies will be low. It's really a reliability/credibility problem. International portfolio managers, who have a limited knowledge of the local scene, will tend to favor those companies which are more forthcoming in terms of their disclosures.

Investors and the Future

When asked whether they planned to increase the scope or extent of their international investments in the future, 11 out of 17 said yes. Attractive growth opportunities outside domestic markets, especially in emerging capital markets, were cited in addition to those mentioned earlier in this study. Of the six respondents who said that accounting diversity did not affect their decisions, two thirds planned to increase the scope of their future investment activities, some suggesting that accounting considerations could become more important in the future.

> As we increase our scale of foreign equity investments, the more we have to know. So far, our need to make foreign investments has been limited and we did not need to know those things (the effects of accounting differences) in detail. But from now on, I personally believe our investments in foreign securities will increase and we will have to know these differences. It must become clearer and clearer.

Are international accounting standards, such as those being promulgated by the International Accounting Standards Committee, viewed as a promising solution to the problems associated with international accounting diversity? Half of those responding said yes; the other half, no. Those who are not bothered by accounting differences generally see no need for international standards. Those in favor of international accounting standards feel that harmonized standards will not only make analysts' lives a little easier but will also enlarge investor interest in international markets.

> The desirability of international accounting standards is a two-edged sword. International standards, on the one hand would erode our comparative advantage in statement analysis. On the other hand, we also cannot survive on the basis of special market knowledge that is not understood by anyone else. There are other markets, other industries, other invest-

ment possibilities. And, we want to be part of a global market not an isolated market. (A)

> While people say they can deal with international accounting differences, there are a whole lot of people out there who really won't touch international securities because they can't deal with accounting differences. If there's global uniformity, the total volume of global investments would expand as more and more investors venture into the international arena. (B)

Those opposed to international accounting standards or who do not believe that international accounting standards offer an improvement over the status quo spoke as follows:

> International accounting standards would not be helpful, because share values are determined by the local market. The local market, in turn, relies on local accounting principles, not international principles. (A)

> To harmonize all the accounting systems around the world, you have to harmonize the incentives for every company and every country for it to make sense. Unless tax systems are harmonized, true harmonization will never happen. (B)

> Harmonization might be so broad in the alternatives permitted as not to make any difference to sophisticated investors. What does matter is the availability of sound audited financial statements. We have been investing in overseas equities for over 30 years and are doing quite well without international standards, thank you, and we are prepared to adjust the financial statements ourselves. Harmonization is likely to be more needed in emerging capital markets. However, there, inflation and currency considerations are more important. (C)

CORPORATE ISSUER RESPONSES

Information Requirements and Accounting Diversity

Corporate issuers rely on a variety of information types when making their international funding decisions. Since their access to foreign markets is conditional upon the provision of some level of financial information about the company, firm specific data is considered a relevant decision input.

All of our corporate issuer interviews were with people closely associated with Treasury operations. All of those surveyed reported that their objectives were to minimize the firm's cost of funding (some added, "on an after-tax basis") or to maximize the value of the equity shares in the firm. Most respondents measured their own performance by looking at the firm's P/E ratio (in relation to competing firms), the firm's cost of capital, or the firm's share price behavior after certain decisions or announcements.

Like the investors in our sample, corporate issuers think of accounting diversity in terms of accounting principles and financial disclosure. However, for many outside the United States, this distinction is blurred. Consider the following exchange with one person in our sample using the help of a language translator:

INTERVIEWER:

Mr. X, what does the term, *accounting diversity* mean to you?

INTERPRETER:

(Laughter) The first thing that comes to the mind of Mr. X is the SEC's reporting requirements.

INTERVIEWER:

What is the second thing that comes to mind?

INTERPRETER:

(More laughter) He can't think of anything else.

In contrast to the investor group, corporate issuers think of accounting diversity as embracing auditing, as well as GAAP and financial disclosure differences. This response was also voiced primarily by issuers outside the United States. In the words of one issuer:

Auditing differences are quite substantial. Unfortunately, here's an area where there's quite a difference in my view between the U.K. and U.S. There's clearly a big difference between the U.K. and France and the U.K. and Germany. To a degree, the disharmony is not quite as bad as one might expect for one reason—because of the impact of the international accounting firms.

Another respondent supplied a much broader interpretation of international accounting diversity, which he said:

. . . starts with differences in philosophy and goes all the way through to the nit-picking differences in record keeping. If you take the three or four systems most clearly derived from the English system (which are the U.S., Canada, and Australia), there aren't really any differences. . . . If you go on from there to the others, which I'm describing as philosophical and cultural differences, you have the Napoleonic code which is in very widespread use still. . . . Then you go to the (and I'm not sure how you describe the German style of accounting) but let's say tax-driven accounting. Those are three fundamental differences between the systems which creates the major diversity.

Accounting Diversity and Issuer Decisions

Most of the issuers in our sample, 14 out of 15, report that GAAP differences have no significant bearing on the measurement of their decision variables. Disclosure differences, in the form of regulatory requirements, however, pose problems for several of the issuers interviewed, primarily those domiciled in Japan and West Germany. One executive lamented:

> The major problem for us is the disclosure requirements of the SEC. So from that point of view, we haven't issued any bonds or stock in the United States, yet. We have preferred to go to the Euromarkets that are very free. We have issued bonds and bonds with warrants of many types. So I don't think there is any important problem in the Euromarket. But in the U.S. market, we are not ready to comply with their requirements.

Disclosure items mentioned most frequently in this regard include preparation of consolidated statements, provision of information on business segments, reporting quarterly results, and explaining the nature of various reserves to foreign analysts. No issuer reported being currently affected by auditing differences, although a few admitted that this was a problem when they first approached the international markets 10 to 15 years earlier.

Consistent with the findings above, nine of the 15 issuers interviewed report that accounting differences have no impact on their funding decisions. Reasons for the noneffect include company funding strategies that insulate the reporting company from reporting to foreign investors, management's focus on economic fundamentals, management's confidence in investors' abilities to deal with accounting differences, the value of name recognition that minimizes the need to focus on accounting considerations, and various coping strategies that have proved effective. Numerous examples of specifics were given:

Owing to our preference for centralized financing and intercompany lending, we cannot identify any impact that foreign accounting or reporting has had on our funding decisions. (A)

One, our financial decisions are taken with a view to the long term only. Two, they are also taken with a view to the economic implications of any decision; not to the accounting results. . . . In my 18 years with our company, I cannot think of a single decision ever taken that was detrimental economically that had a favorable accounting result. Conversely, we have never been deterred from doing something because it had an adverse accounting result. (B)

We have talked to a number of investment directors directly. They have been quite candid and said that whether we have or haven't an ADR traded abroad is totally irrelevant. Whether the company is reporting its financial results according to GAAP is equally totally irrelevant. They know the differences and can make the adjustments if they want to make the adjustment to read the foreign accounts. It's not a problem actually. (C)

The Japanese are very good at doing their homework. More than other countries. . . . They're more uncertain about a non-Japanese investment and that probably drives them to be more thorough. But, of course, most of them have got their London or European offices now, and they've got a lot of non-Japanese people doing their work for them. So there's a lot of bridging of that kind going on. There is obviously some problem around and that is that investors tend to feel more comfortable with accounting conventions they're more familiar with. I don't know how big a problem that is. . . . But again, I come back to the specialization. A man who is more likely to be looking at our company is going to be a man familiar with our country. (D)

We're largely dealing with sophisticated investors, and we get very little complaint about [accounting differences]. We've never had issues of "what would this be in French terms" or "what would this be in German terms." We're dealing with global investors, and they understand [accounting differences]. I'm not saying that there is not a minor barrier, but it's not one that ever seems to create problems. (E)

A significant minority, six out of 15 issuers, report that their financial decisions are affected by accounting differences. Of the six, one has made a conscious decision to court sophisticated investors that can deal with accounting diversity, three have avoided accessing the U.S. capital market, and two have altered their investor relations programs as a means of enhancing their share values and, ultimately, their financing terms. The following quotations illustrate this type of behavior.

The investors we're trying to attract to buy our shares are investors who are going to take a long-term view and are reasonably sophisticated in terms of investing in a business that is in fact international in terms of its risk. That more or less means that you're going to be looking for investors who aren't domestic investors; they're going to be international investors who are capable of investing in Japan as much as they are in investing in New York, London, or anywhere else. (A)

Our accounting treatment for certain intangibles significantly affects our reported net worth. As a consequence, we have not been able to get a credit rating from the major rating agencies. Thus far, we have not attempted to raise funds in the U.S. but have floated commercial paper in Europe instead. . . . If we decide to go to the U.S. market, we will restate to U.S. GAAP. (B)

We must do everything we can to maximize shareholder value. Financial engineering helps to maximize share values, because investors respond positively to accounting measurements which exceed domestic standards. (C)

We find no correlation between these results and either organizational structure or funding philosophy. We do, however, observe a correlation between decision effects with country of origin, firm size, length of international funding experience, and geographical scope of external sourcing activities. This is illustrated in Table 14.

All four North American issuers report "no impact" of accounting diversity on their financial decisions. In contrast, most non-U.S. listers, with the exception of those who have been grandfathered (having previously issued American Depositary Receipts in the United States) or who are cash rich and in no need of external funds, report an impact of accounting diversity on their financing decisions.

In our sample, most large firms report they are not affected by accounting diversity, the exceptions being a large Japanese and a large German firm. Firms of lesser size, however, tend to report that they are affected by accounting differences. The exceptions were two less large North American firms.

Firms with long experience in international financial markets tend to say they are not affected by accounting diversity. The exceptions here were one Japanese and two German firms. Firms with short experience more often than not said they were affected by international accounting diversity. A large cash-rich firm with short experience was an exception.

Finally, firms that have engaged in extensive international funding arrangements tend to say they are not affected by accounting diversity, as opposed to those whose funding activities have been more limited in scope. The exceptions to the former were two Japanese firms that have made extensive use of the Eurobond markets and non-U.S. equity listings. Exceptions to the latter were three firms that have accessed few markets but have come to the U.S. market on earlier occasions.

Issuer Coping Mechanisms

Corporate issuers who said that accounting differences had no affect on their funding decisions, nine of 16, cope in a variety of ways. One non-U.S. issuer copes by restating its accounts to a U.S. basis. In this instance, switching to U.S. GAAP has the effect of casting statements in a more positive light. Two issuers cope by partially restating their accounts from domestic to U.S. accounting principles. In one case, the company had been grandfathered in the U.S. and did not have to fully conform to U.S. GAAP restatements.[5] In the other case, partial restatement to U.S. GAAP made the company's operating income appear more favorable but did not affect its bottom line one way or the other. On the matter of restatement, one issuer is very reluctant to use restatement as a coping mechanism. He cautions:

> I am very reluctant to restate my accounting principles for the convenience of the foreign reader. For example, the German Financial Analysts Association has devised a way to arrive at a more realistic earnings figure for German companies. First, they eliminate all extraordinary items and discretionary and accounting reserves. The result is divided by shares outstanding. However, the resulting number is not equal to U.S. earnings per share. So, restatement has the potential to change the message of the original number.

Three of the nine issuers cope by going on roadshows and hosting analysts meetings. Three cope by essentially doing nothing. In the latter case, all three companies happen to be North American firms that enjoy reciprocity when raising funds in foreign capital markets. Non-U.S. reg-

---

[5]In 1982, the U.S. Securities and Exchange Commission grandfathered foreign firms listed on U.S. stock exchanges, exempting them from SEC reporting requirements, provided they did not raise capital in the United States.

ulators generally respect the accounting principles of the issuer's home country.

There are additional reasons that appear to partly explain the immunity of this segment of the issuing sample to accounting effects. Five of the nine issuers had previously floated new equity issues in the United States. Two had issued ADRs in the U.S. market that had been grandfathered from having to meet more stringent U.S. reporting requirements. Finally, two were large, cash-rich firms that were not dependent on external sourcing for their funding needs.

Capital market effects stemming from accounting diversity were negligible for this group. Four respondents reported that accounting diversity affected their information preparation costs. Of the four, only one respondent reported that the information cost was significant. In this case, the benefits reportedly exceeded the costs.

Corporate issuers who say their funding decisions are affected by accounting differences also attempt to cope with such differences. Accounting coping takes the form of partial GAAP restatements for three of the six members of this issuer segment. In these cases, full restatement would have made one issuer appear to be less well-off than before. The other two would look much better under full restatement, given the conservative reporting practices in their home countries. However, both were unwilling to go the full route, as full restatements would increase their competitive costs. The other three members of this issuer group used road shows or hosted analysts' meetings to answer questions relating to accounting or disclosure issues. For two of the three issuers, restatement to U.S. GAAP would make them look better but would reveal privileged information to competitors. Restatement for the third issuer would have made it look less profitable.

The six issuers composing our "yes, accounting diversity is a problem" group also cope in a financial sense. All have avoided raising funds or listing their shares in the U.S. market by either (1) by-passing the U.S. market for the Eurobond market (two companies), (2) relying on domestic bank financing as opposed to floating commercial paper in the United States (one company), (3) encouraging foreign investors to come to their financial market to buy their shares locally (one company), (4) offering sponsored but unlisted ADRs in the United States (two companies), or (5) undertaking a U.S. private placement (one company).

Coping with audit differences generally takes the form of having an audit performed by a major international accounting firm. In many cases this is in addition to a local attestation. As one issuer explains:

> If you want to do international financing, you can't do cherry-picking. You have to offer investors international standards of auditing.

For the six companies described above, accounting diversity is associated with capital market effects (see Table 15). That effect, in turn, relates to the company's cost of capital. The issuers were either unwilling or unable to quantify the magnitude of the effect, but as the following quotes indicate, accounting differences can produce both positive and negative market effects.

> Several years ago we pioneered the practice of disclosing a condensed balance sheet in the regular financial section of the balance sheet, and in an appendix, a more detailed balance sheet in which the accounting is essentially equivalent to U.S. norms. . . . Our P/E ratio is currently more than twice that of our major competitor, and we feel it is due to our accounting and investor relations policy. (A)

> We have probably paid more to obtain external capital in the international markets owing to our reluctance to disclose certain items of information which we view as proprietary. However, in terms of the history of corporate practices in our country, this is not considered a major concern. (B)

Issuers and the Future

Do the corporate issuers in our study plan to increase the extent or geographic scope of their funding or listing activities in the future? "It all depends" was the most common response. Those answering in the affirmative said the underlying motivation was to fund their expanding foreign investments abroad. Those who had no plans to source internationally either had no need for external funding, felt that some foreign markets were over-regulated and overly costly, or could as easily raise funds locally by wooing international investors to purchase their shares in their home markets.

Corporate issuers do not see international accounting standards as a promising remedy to the problems of accounting diversity. Of the issuers who responded positively to the notion of international standards, many did so with tongue in cheek, as the following testimonials indicate.

Having an international set of accounting standards would be a good idea, but we won't see it in our lifetimes. (A)

We are very interested in the initiative of the SEC and the International Organization of Securities Commissions (IOSCO) which has as its goal truly international securities trading. This will be accomplished, eventually, by requiring the adoption of uniform international accounting standards. Obviously, we are concerned that these new standards parallel, or at least be consistent with, U.S. accounting standards. (B)

I think the movement to have some sort of harmonization of accounting standards across countries is a noble undertaking as long as it's not done by the FASB. (C)

Those opposed to international accounting standards advance the following arguments for their positions:

I believe that what will happen will not be a harmonizing or an international conformity in accounting. What will come will be reciprocity between exchanges. The American exchanges will accept listing requirements of other exchanges. There will be some harmonizing of listing requirements, but I don't think it will necessarily go to the accounting. It might go to some reconciliation, but it won't go much farther than that. (A)

Any discussion of international standards is helpful. But, to expect that it will change the way we account for our business is unrealistic. (B)

It is Mr. X's opinion that there is no difference between U.S. GAAP and international GAAP. So he feels that a U.S. GAAP basis is still preferable. (C)

I feel that reciprocity is coming. If the SEC's disclosure requirements are too high, it will discourage foreign issuers and my company from selling shares in the United States. This will force U.S. investors to purchase foreign shares abroad where they are less protected by disclosure requirements. So, I think that the SEC will have to modify its disclosure requirements. (D)

UNDERWRITER RESPONSES

Underwriters play an important role in facilitating capital market transactions by matching investor demands for securities that satisfy a spectrum of risk-return preferences, with corporate issuers in search of external sources of capital. In practice, both institutional investors and corporate issuers may rely heavily on advice from financial intermediaries for all dimensions of a capital market decision. For example, the amount, timing, currency of denomination, and location for a new public offering, the decision of an equity, debt, or hybrid issue, and the decision regarding listing of an existing or planned security are all decisions on which the advice of underwriters might be sought. Therefore, the potential effect of accounting diversity upon underwriting decisions is an important concern for the operation of international capital markets.

Information Requirements and Accounting Diversity

Categories of information relied on by underwriters cover a wide range. All of the underwriters in our sample rely on market, firm-specific, macroeconomic, political, regulatory and tax information as a basis for their decisions. The eight underwriters in our sample generally associate the term *accounting diversity* with differences in accounting principles, financial disclosure, and external auditing.

Accounting Diversity and Underwriter Decisions

Seven of the eight underwriters interviewed say that national accounting principles differences affect their underwriting decisions. The respondent for which accounting differences are not a problem commented:

> Accounting differences are not a major issue for us at the level of the world class issuers that we deal with. At that level, name recognition and credit rating dominate. However, as you come down the scale or deal with private placements or credit analysis, the issue of accounting differences becomes more important.

Countries whose accounting principles are most frequently cited as proving troublesome are Germany and Switzerland. Banks and insurance companies were cited as industries in which accounting differences are most pronounced. Specific measurement rules that were noted as a source of dissatisfaction include accounting for consolidated accounts, inventory, foreign currency translation and transactions, provisions for bad debts, long-term contracts, contingencies, depreciation, goodwill, leases, and marketable securities. Since only one underwriter responded that accounting diversity had no effect on his decisions, correlation of the patterns of responses with organizational characteristics such as size, length of experience, nationality, and so forth is not meaningful.

While most underwriters are not bothered by audit differences, in some countries disclosure differences are troublesome. In our interviews, Italy, Portugal, Japan, Spain, Switzerland, and countries with capital markets in the early stages of development were cited as troublesome. However, concern over disclosure differences is not confined to countries with emerging capital markets. The United States and the United Kingdom were also identified in this group of countries with troublesome disclosure differences.[6] Disclosure items that were highlighted in our interviews as a source of dissatisfaction relate to business segments, comparative financial statements, interim statements, funds flow, identification of accounting policies, forecasts, related party transactions, off-balance sheet financing, and details of capital structure.

Underwriter Coping Mechanisms

Underwriters cope with accounting diversity, both accounting principles and disclosure, in a variety of ways. The respondent who is not bothered by accounting differences copes by (1) soliciting only the top-tier firms in the industry, (2) relying on credit ratings, and (3) accessing foreign capital via private placements. Underwriters who are concerned with accounting differences cope in both an accounting and nonaccounting sense. Coping with accounting principles differences takes the form of (1) restating foreign accounts to local GAAP (five respondents), (2) restating foreign accounts to both local GAAP and U.S. GAAP (one), or (3) examining rates of change in original accounting data (one). While restatement is a common practice, one underwriter does not stop there. In his words:

> Restatement is helpful but not sufficient. Accounts which are prepared by accountants are true, but they may not be all the truth. It is important to understand the local cultural and business norms as a basis for properly interpreting the restated numbers.

Coping with disclosure differences manifests itself in the form of (1) requests for additional information (five underwriters), (2) obtaining guarantees from the parent company or some third party (one), or (3) avoiding the U.S. market in favor of a less demanding market (two).

---

[6]Troublesome disclosure differences in this context refer to accounting and financial disclosure requirements that are more demanding than that of the client's country of origin.

Accounting differences, in turn, are associated with capital market effects. These effects are summarized in Table 16. An example of a specific market effect is offered in the following quote:

> I think any company should think five times before getting caught with a U.S. quote and the requirement to produce quarterly profits [statements]. Damned expensive! And, there is no benefit at all, because the few U.S. investors who invest internationally won't be interested whether it is quoted in New York or not. I would always advise my clients not to have a quote in New York unless you're prepared to spend a huge amount of money. If you want to produce quarterly reports, that's fine. But the opinion of the rest of the world is that production of quarterly reports is not helpful; half-yearly is quite enough.

Underwriters and the Future

With one exception, all underwriters plan to increase the level or international scope of their underwriting activities in the future, including the underwriter whose decisions were not affected by accounting differences. In his words:

> We will soon begin to look at the next tier of firms that we do not presently consider. The motivating factor is that there is no money to be made servicing the large corporates. The only reason we do it is for the prestige these days. And, the smaller the issuer the greater the scope for charging genuine fees.

Another underwriter explained the enhanced importance of the international dimension in terms of the classic "hog cycle," but in this case applied to the market for information. In the hog cycle, the supply of hogs in one season follows from the price in the previous season. High prices stimulate high production, low prices stimulate little production, and so the market tends to go through boom and bust cycles.

In financial markets, one underwriter argued, there may be a hog cycle for information. When the level of information collection is low, markets may appear inefficient and there will be a high return from collecting information. As other people observe that there is a return on that information, they too start collecting information. Eventually, the market becomes fairly saturated with information, and the return from collecting information begins to fall. However, the market can detect this change in returns only with a lag. Since people continue to collect information until the returns from collecting information are less than the cost, the market reaches a point of oversupply of information. In this stage of the cycle, it will be difficult to use information to outperform the market. The demand for index-like funds rises, and a shakeout occurs leading to a decline in information collected. At some point, the return on collecting information starts to increase, and the whole cycle starts again.

The link to the international capital market is that all national markets may not be in the same stage of the cycle at the same time. The job for underwriters is to identify which capital markets are over- or under-supplied with information, that is, where prices for either institutional investors or corporate issuers are most favorable. According to the underwriter espousing this theory, the U.S. and U.K. markets were at the oversupply of information stage, making the international markets more attractive for investments. In his words:

> The domestic markets are at the stage of the hog cycle where it's increasingly difficult to outperform the index. But, in the international market, you can enjoy much higher returns to information. Accounting differences, in this context, provide underwriters with an opportunity, because they act as a barrier to entry. One of the reasons why the domestic fund management business in the United States has been so awful during the past 10 years is because there have been too many boutique entrants.
>
> The thing that's nice about international fund management is that the boutiques can't do it. The range of skills that are required, in terms of linguistic skills, accounting skills, and the like are too extensive for many to compete; the number of countries and companies to monitor is immense. This is where large organizations enjoy a comparative advantage owing to economies of scale.
>
> As far as we're concerned, we regard the accounting differences as working in our favor. The superior returns which we are able to get from international investing is related to the fact that the international markets are less perfect than the national markets. Therefore we believe you can improve your returns through management more in the international markets than you can within the national market.

Another investor expressed essentially the same opinion:

> When I look at the American market which is *so* efficient, in a way it has become a difficult market. Whereas in Europe, there is still room not for insider information, but there is a value assigned to well-conducted

research efforts by portfolio managers. And these efforts can have very good yields.

Underwriters are divided on the desirability of international accounting standards. One underwriter who favors the notion of a single set of accounting standards states:

> Maybe if you did have one common accounting standard, then issuing houses such as ourselves and investors would feel that much more comfortable in talking about new names who we've sort of automatically dismissed for the moment through a combination of factors. It would also greatly facilitate comparisons of new names with more established names.

Another underwriter favored harmonization, but primarily of the sort proposed for the European Community (EC). In his opinion:

> Accounting harmonization associated with the planned 1992 European integration will be a good thing. On the one hand, it will be more difficult for German companies, especially banks, who will have to provide consolidated statements for the first time. On the other hand, it will make company accounts more transparent. This, in turn, will enable analysts to measure company size and earnings on a more uniform basis.

Another underwriter who prefers national accounting principles pointed out the hidden dangers in international standards:

> International accounting standards are not necessarily superior to national standards. Indeed, you can think of them as a form of cultural imperialism. Politics aside, there is a danger that international standards delude the unsophisticated investor into thinking that you've genuinely harmonized. It may, in fact, be healthy to have things look a little different, because it makes people realize that there are some differences. We regard national accounts, even when they're audited by the major international auditing firms, as meaning different things in different countries.

REGULATOR RESPONSES

Market regulators deal with three major constituencies—investors, corporate issuers, and organized exchanges that facilitate the transfer of securities between the former and the latter. Most of the regulatory bodies we interviewed had as their major objectives the protection of investors, creation of a level playing field for issuers of debt and equity securities, and assurance that security transactions are effected efficiently and fairly.

All of the eight regulatory bodies we interviewed require foreign issuers or listers to submit audited financial statements as a condition for capital market entry. Accordingly, regulators generally associated accounting measurement principles, the extent of financial disclosure, and audit practices with the term *accounting diversity*.

Accounting Diversity and Regulatory Decisions

While one might expect the decisions of this survey group to be affected by accounting diversity, especially among those whose experience with international transactions has been relatively short, we found this not to be the case. With the exception of one regulatory agency, none reported being hindered by accounting principles differences when attempting to measure their decision variables. Neither was any regulator bothered by national disclosure or auditing differences.

Consistent with the foregoing responses, all regulators were able to successfully cope with such differences, and in no case were decisions with respect to new issues or listing of foreign securities affected by accounting diversity. Of the various coping mechanisms used, the United States was alone in requiring foreign issuers/listers to reconcile their national accounting principles to U.S. GAAP. The following testimonials provide some insight into the nature of other adaptive behavior.

> Foreign company financial statements based on mother country accounting principles are acceptable to us. The merit of accepting the foreign-practice accounting statements is that the local investor will receive the same information as the foreign country's investor. (A)
>
> An application for a foreign listing or new issue in our market must be filed by the issuer and at least one sponsoring bank. Since the sponsoring bank has some burden of responsibility in bringing a foreign issuer to our capital market, it is expected to have examined the financial status of the company before proposing a listing/new issue. That is, the material examination of a foreign issuer is performed by the sponsoring bank. (B)
>
> We rely on market forces to deal with the issue of international accounting diversity. Investment advisors who cannot cope with accounting differences will give poorer investment advice than those who can. We do not feel that government should step in and deal with a problem that the market is better equipped to deal with. (C)

When the accounts of a foreign lister/issuer are prepared on a basis that is significantly different than our own, we require the adoption of IASC standards as a minimum. (D)

Because of our long experience in international investments, we have basically sensitized ourselves to many foreign environments—their languages, their way of thinking, and their systems of accounting too. Thus, we do not feel a need to restate foreign accounts to domestic accounting principles. Rather we look at a set of foreign financial statements based on its own set of accounting principles and attempt to glean the message contained therein within the context of its own environment. (E)

Because of the nature of their organizations, most regulators coped with disclosure differences simply by requesting additional information. Second audit opinions were requested in those instances where auditor qualifications or audit procedures were in doubt.

While accounting differences did impose additional information processing costs on market regulators, this cost was not considered significant. Two regulators indicated, however, that disclosure differences had some adverse effect in the volume of foreign issuing or listing activities conducted in their national jurisdictions. One acknowledged the loss of foreign issuers or listers to markets requiring less extensive disclosure practices. The second, on the other hand, expressed concern that excessive leniency produced similar capital market effects by reducing investor confidence in its market.

Regulators and the Future

Most of the regulators we spoke to expected an increase in the level or scope of their regulatory activities with respect to international securities in the future. The recent surge in leveraged buy-outs and merger and acquisition activities is reducing the number of domestic shares that are listed or traded on domestic exchanges. Accordingly, new listings and capital market issues will come from the international arena. The stock market crash of 1987 has also caused investors to shy away from markets with loose regulatory structures. In the words of one regulator:

While the investor constituency is still weak in our country, it is growing at an accelerating rate, and institutional investors are an important element of the local investment scene. We don't want to lose this business.

In the words of another regulator:

> Pressure for greater corporate transparency is increasing all the time. The pressure is coming from the providers of capital.

Moreover, the move by the European Community to remove existing barriers to the integration of its capital markets by the end of 1992 and the focus on accounting and disclosure as part of that integration are creating a demonstration effect in capital markets elsewhere. Thus, it is felt that many countries are planning to move closer to EC norms.

Market regulators are divided on the desirability of adopting international accounting standards. Those not in favor of international accounting standards (four of seven respondents) offer several reasons for their position. One prefers the notion of reciprocity to harmonization. Under reciprocity, each securities exchange or regulatory body agrees to accept the accounting, financial disclosure, and audit practices of the foreign issuer's/lister's home country. Ease of implementation and flexibility are cited as desirable attributes of this option. Another regulator prefers to have each country strengthen its national standards, as opposed to having them conform to some arbitrary norm that generally reflects some minimum acceptable standard. Still another favors accounting harmonization along the lines being pursued by the European Community as these EC standards (directives) have the force of law behind them rather than voluntary compliance. Finally, a fourth regulator was opposed to international accounting standards, as there is no evidence that institutional investors or security analysts pay any attention to them.

Several of the regulators voicing support for harmonized accounting standards did so in equivocal terms. In a poor display of harmony and diplomacy, one regulator commented:

> We are in favor of international accounting standards as long as they conform to *our* accounting standards.

Another regulator credited the quest for international accounting standards to market forces. In particular, he felt that competition among national regulators for an optimum share of the burgeoning market for international issues, rather than the merit or logic of IASC pronouncements, was the principle driving force for accounting harmonization. A third regulator's response, while appearing facetious on the surface, was not intended as such. We quote him directly.

Administrators like myself and stock exchange people are big promoters of such things as International Accounting Standards and the IASC. We tend to love discussing such topics. However, if I listen to the people I work for, they do not care about such activities. Of course there are aspects of harmonization that would be nice to have. But after all, they're making their money from it.

OTHER SURVEY RESPONSES

To round out our interviews, we surveyed two final categories of international accounting statement readers: first, organizations that specialize in rating the debt instruments of both domestic and international corporate issuers, and second, fee-based financial information services. Ratings of the former group are conditional, in part, on information contained in a borrower's accounting-based financial statements and can significantly affect the cost and terms of external funding. The inclusion of this user group adds another perspective on the capital market effects of international accounting differences.

All respondents in this user category found differences in national accounting principles to be a hindrance when attempting to measure their decision-variables. As one respondent explains:

Ten years ago, our primary readership was a U.S. audience. Today, it is to a great extent a rating for an international product that is targeted for an international market. This has come about because of the recent explosion in Eurobond and Eurocommercial paper offerings by companies in the U.S., Europe, and Asia, that are aimed at truly international investors. Moreover, these international issuers are no longer brand names such as ICI or Siemens—it's a lot of companies who investors don't know, and we're frankly a little worried about this.

Our big concern has always been—especially when we're running all of this out of New York—which is the relevant standard of comparison? There's nothing that will turn a company off more than to think they are being analyzed by American analysts on American accounting standards to satisfy an American rating scale. We've tried to internationalize ourselves; we've had to to get international issuers to approach us for ratings. One of our big problems is that there just isn't the SEC, there isn't the disclosure, there isn't the information. So we've had to rely on domestic sources for the counts, the projections, for a lot of the financial information. This has raised some tough rating issues.

Countries whose accounting principles proved most troublesome included Australia, France, Switzerland, and West Germany. Specific industries mentioned along similar lines were chemicals and financial services. GAAP items identified as the cause of such difficulties include consolidated accounts, inventory valuation, discretionary reserves, leases, long-term construction contracts, foreign exchange gains and losses, and the estimation of pension costs and asset values.

Countries whose disclosure practices were found wanting included Switzerland and West Germany in particular. Specific disclosure items mentioned included segmental disclosures, details of financial statement items (provisioning), details of capital structure, off-balance-sheet disclosures, pending litigation, and disclosures relating to the estimation of oil and gas reserves.

While respondents in our sample responded similarly with respect to the measurement effects of accounting differences, such was not the case for decision effects. The respondent reporting no effects of accounting diversity on its decisions coped by examining trend statistics versus absolute levels when examining financial statement data and by relying on local accounting measurement rules. Respondents whose decisions are affected by accounting differences cope by restating. In one instance, the respondent restates foreign accounts to the reporting principles of its country-of-domicile. The other respondent restates foreign accounting principles into a set of in-house measurement standards that he believes possess more information content than either foreign accounting principles or those of the respondent's country.

Responses regarding capital market effects of accounting diversity were consistent with reported decision effects. The respondent whose rating decisions were insensitive to accounting differences attributed no location, information, or valuation effects to such differences. The other respondent, for which this question is pertinent, reported that accounting and reporting differences did affect security values by way of differential debt ratings assigned.

In terms of the future, all three respondents in this category plan to increase the level and geographic scope of their respective activities. They are generally not, however, in favor of having a common set of accounting rules promulgated by an international accounting standards committee. One respondent was opposed to a common set of accounting standards on the grounds that adherence to a single set of measurement rules would not reduce its information processing costs, as it would still have to translate accounts prepared according to "generally accepted international standards" to its own reporting norms. Another respondent argues that the international capital market will evolve its own set of reporting standards. The third respondent expressed his views as follows:

> While international accounting principles may be desired by investors, the first thing that needs to be harmonized is the extent of corporate financial disclosure. Even if national accounting principles are different, as long as a company discloses what it does, an investor can reconcile the differences for himself based on his own restatement algorithm.

CHAPTER 6

SURVEY CONCLUSIONS

CONCLUSIONS REGARDING INVESTORS, ACCOUNTING DIVERSITY, AND CAPITAL MARKET EFFECTS

A significant proportion of investors (9 of 17) in our sample report that international accounting diversity, in terms of accounting principles and financial disclosure differences, affects their investment decisions. For these respondents, accounting diversity is a problem that leads to capital market effects ranging from the geographic location where investments are made to the valuation of foreign equities. Auditing differences do not appear to be a subject of much concern as long as audits are performed by a reputable firm.[1]

All who deal with national accounting differences cope in some fashion. For a significant number of investors, coping takes the form of restating foreign accounting numbers to the reporting principles of the investor's country-of-domicile or to a set of accounting standards that are internationally recognized. In our sample, *all* who attempt to restate foreign accounting information report that accounting diversity affects their investment decisions. In other words, restatement is *not* sufficient to remove the problem of accounting diversity.

This finding suggests that either (*a*) existing restatement algorithms have not been perfected, (*b*) existing algorithms are not being applied effectively, or (*c*) no algorithm is capable of producing a proper and meaningful restatement. Whether restatement fails to be an adequate coping mechanism because of (*a*), (*b*), or (*c*) is obviously critical. If the reason is (*a*) or (*b*), then more effort in restatement will result in a

---

[1]Most of our respondents associated reputation with size and an international capability.

payoff. If the true reason is (c), then investors may be right in developing their skills to read and interpret foreign financial statements in their
original form.

In our sample, facility in dealing with multiple sets of accounting
principles, multiple principles capabilities (MPC), is relatively uncom-
mon. Only four of seventeen firms relied on original unrestated data for
their investment decisions. Interestingly, but perhaps not surprisingly,
none of the respondents that were MPCers reported that accounting diversity poses a problem as far as their investment decisions are concerned. In our sample, development of an MPC approach appears to be
a sufficient (but not a necessary condition) for a respondent to claim that
accounting diversity has no impact on investment decisions.

On the other hand, a segment of those who report not being affected by accounting diversity may not be coping in an optimal fashion.
Consider the following statement by an investor who copes with accounting diversity by adopting a top-down investment strategy:

> I would also like to see data bases for European companies improved
> as well as a narrowing of GAAP differences. Would I purchase a global
> data base in which company accounts were restated to U.S. GAAP or
> some third-country GAAP if it were available? Very definitely. [Col-
> league speaks] This is what we are all waiting for. Indeed, if such data
> were available, we would seriously consider organizing ourselves along
> industry lines as we were in the early years. . . . If you look at the typical
> analyst in the States and compare him with the typical analyst in Europe,
> the American analyst has much information available to him on American
> companies à la Compustat and others. A European analyst has to go out
> and try to collect the data. If the accounting standards were improved and
> the companies disclosed more, the European analyst could start at the
> same starting point as the U.S. analyst. For me, it would be very interest-
> ing to see what a company like Nestle would look like if it reported
> according to U.S. accounting standards. [Colleague speaks] I think that
> when such data bases are available, then you will see an impact of ac-
> counting differences on the market.

Both investor groups, those who were and were not bothered by
financial disclosure differences, adopt similar approaches in coping with
such diversity. Accordingly, disclosure cannot be used to explain our
observed pattern of responses in the "no problem" versus "problem"
groups. Moreover, visits by investors with corporate officials intended
to obtain further disclosures and explanations may not be sufficient to

remove the problem of accounting diversity for certain investors. In the words of one investor:

> I believe that the real problem is with accounting principles differences. That is, if a company provides lots of disclosure but the company has a lot of leeway in managing what is disclosed, then the picture that is generated is highly unreliable. The two problems [principles and disclosure] are closely related; that is, the errors are highly correlated.

Most of the investors we interviewed are planning to increase the scope of their international investing activities. Many of those who provided a negative reply did so because they felt they were already well-diversified internationally. If these sample responses are indicative of the larger population, it appears that the present extent of accounting diversity is not sufficient to halt institutional investors from continuing to expand their activities.

Investors appear evenly divided as to whether international accounting standards are necessary or will offer a feasible solution to the transnational reporting problem. When asked if there were any preconditions that would entice an organization to expand the geographical scope or extent of its international equity investments, no one voluntarily mentioned the need for a harmonized set of accounting standards.

CONCLUSIONS REGARDING ISSUERS, ACCOUNTING DIVERSITY, AND CAPITAL MARKET EFFECTS

Forty percent of the corporate issuers in our sample say that accounting diversity affects their financial decisions. For these respondents, accounting diversity is a phenomenon that leads to capital market effects.

Most issuers interviewed do not feel that differences in accounting measurement rules affect the measurement of their decision variables. Nevertheless, the impact of disclosure differences on financing decisions is non-neutral. This suggests that accounting diversity and regulatory diversity are closely linked issues from the standpoint of corporate issuers. For example, most firms outside the United States view the Financial Accounting Standards Board (FASB) and the U.S. Securities and Exchange Commission (SEC) as parts of the same regulatory apparatus.[2]

Large issuers with extensive experience in international finance appear to be less associated with problems caused by accounting differences than otherwise. While there are exceptions, it appears that firms that are venturing into the international capital markets or that are relatively inexperienced stand to benefit from advice on how to effectively deal with such differences.

Nationality also seems to play a role in explaining issuer behavior. U.S. and U.K. firms, whose standards of accounting and financial disclosure tend to be relatively high, appear to have more flexibility in accessing international capital markets. On the other hand, German, Japanese, and Swiss firms, whose financial statements are less transparent in the areas of segmental disclosures and hidden reserves, appear to have less flexibility in accessing certain capital markets.

This phenomenon, however, may also be related to the asymmetry we observe between the United States and other countries in our sample with regard to financial market regulation. Market regulation in the United States is based on national treatment.[3] Other countries embrace reciprocity in accepting the accounting and reporting practices of the issuer's mother country. Consequently, U.S. issuers are able to present their financial statements to regulatory bodies abroad and have them evaluated on their own merits.

In short, non-U.S. regulators behave as MPCers. This may explain why no American firms in our sample felt accounting issues raised difficulties for them in tapping international capital markets. In contrast, the United States insists on national treatment (full U.S. GAAP and U.S.-style disclosure) for public offerings and listed securities.[4] This posture

---

[2]Since the SEC's adoption of an integrated disclosure system philosophy in 1980, similarities between the financial statement requirements for general reporting purposes and the financial statement requirements for SEC filings have increased. Specifically, the integration rules encourage conformance of the primary financial disclosure items found in published annual reports with those required in SEC filings.

[3]At the time of this writing, the U.S. Securities and Exchange Commission was considering application of the reciprocity principle on a limited basis, starting with Canada.

[4]Non-U.S. issuers are free to approach the U.S. private placement market with their original accounting reports, but because of restrictions on resale, issuers have faced higher costs. Rule

imposes additional costs on non-U.S. issuers, and some are not willing to bear these costs.

For issuers, it is important to distinguish between their financial decisions and the capital market effect of these decisions. In the case of investors, positive or negative signals conveyed by reported accounting numbers cause them to either raise or lower their assessments of firm value and, hence, the price at which they will trade a share of stock. In short, their decisions are translated directly into capital market effects. In the case of corporate issuers, however, decisions with respect to accounting principles employed, amount of information publicly conveyed, class of external auditor engaged, financial market selected, type of financing instrument chosen, investor group targeted, and so forth are all decisions that only indirectly affect the market price of its shares and, hence, its capital costs. The capital market effects of the decisions just described are the result of how firm decisions affect the pricing decisions of various market agents (e.g., banks, rating agencies, investors).

In the latter regard, issuers differ from investors in yet another respect. Investors are generally concerned with a single object, namely, the entity whose shares they wish to trade. Corporate issuers, on the other hand, face a number of constituencies. They include, but are not limited to, investors (both domestic and foreign), rating agencies, domestic regulators (e.g., tax authorities, regulatory bodies, labor unions), and foreign regulators (primarily securities market officials). Accordingly, the firm must be sensitive to information needs of each group and may attempt to tailor the information provided to the needs of each audience-of-interest (e.g., supply special information to ratings agencies on a confidential basis, arrange special presentations to financial analysts, comply with the accounting and reporting requirements of foreign stock market officials, and the like). All firms, in turn, attempt a more or less constrained optimization with each constituency. The net result of this financial engineering will ultimately be reflected in its

---

144A and Regulation S, approved on April 19, 1990, will remove many of these resale restrictions for large institutional investors ($100 million or more under management). In principle, a large liquid "144A market" could emerge for nonregistered securities issued by non-U.S. firms. This would reduce the distinction between private placements and public offerings. Accounting principles and disclosure standards would be determined by market forces rather than SEC regulations. For a more detailed discussion, see Aaron S. Gurwitz, *SEC Rule 144A and Regulation S: Impact on Global Fixed Income Markets*, Fixed Income Research Series (New York: Goldman Sachs, 1989).

share price. Thus, competitive costs (such as an attempted hostile take-over) may encourage the release of information to raise share values. Other competitive concerns (such as U.S. trade action against suspected dumping) may suggest a strategy of limiting segmental disclosures. Thus, corporate issuers must face and deal with many more decision points than is normally assumed. According to one issuer:

> The name of the game today is financial marketing! You have to tell investors what you're going to do, what are the opportunities. Then, you have to give them an annual report every 12 months to show them that you did perform as you promised previously. If you don't understand this cycle, you can make a glorious presentation at a board meeting as to what a sponsored or unsponsored ADR program will do for you. But whether it actually has a favorable impact on your financing, I say no.

All firms in our sample stated that their objective function (as far as treasury is concerned) is to maximize the value of the firm and to minimize their cost of capital. To better understand corporate behavior, we find it useful to interpret *cost minimization* in a broad manner. Typically, the finance literature models a firm's cost of capital solely as a function of its financial cost (perhaps on an after-tax basis and in terms of a particular currency). In the context of this study, the total cost of raising funds may be modeled as a function of (1) financial costs, (2) information preparation costs, and (3) competitive costs.

In communicating with foreign readers who are used to a different accounting and reporting framework, firms can restate local GAAP statements into the accounting principles of the reader's country-of-domicile, supply additional disclosures, and/or have the audit report reflect an enhanced set of auditing standards. At the margin, additional information should lower the financial costs to the firm. But additional information is costly to prepare and may also increase the competitive costs to the firm. Thus, the firm will provide that amount of information that optimizes the trade-off between competitive costs and financial costs. Especially in countries where the firm can submit only one statement of accounts—rather than separate statements for external reporting, tax purposes, regulatory agencies, and so forth—the question of which accounting figures to release reflects a careful balancing act.

We find this framework helpful in explaining the corporate decision effects of accounting diversity and coping behavior that we observed. For example, it helps to explain why some firms are willing only to partially restate from one set of accounting standards to another, while others are willing to undertake more comprehensive restatements. It helps one to understand why some firms are willing to restate domestic GAAP statements to another set of accounting principles, while others are willing to disclose more but unwilling to undertake GAAP restatements. It also helps to rationalize corporate behavior that avoids any form of accounting coping in favor of purely financial strategies, that is, firms using firm-specific advantages (such as the value of their name recognition) to avoid compliance with costly regulation by going to the Euromarkets.

Country of origin plays a role in our model of total cost minimization. Issuers from a country with substantial accounting disclosure (e.g., the United Kingdom) will be more concerned about the impact of GAAP differences on their competitive costs. Issuers from a country with limited disclosures (e.g., Germany and Japan) will be more concerned about the competitive costs of additional disclosure.

Based on the observed coping behavior of various corporate issuers, it appears that some non-U.S. firms have avoided problems related to accounting diversity by reason of their size and name recognition, their ability to generate funds internally (i.e., cash rich), or by the good fortune of being grandfathered into the U.S. market.

Demand for international accounting standards does not seem to be emanating from the corporate world. In view of the multiple constituencies with which a company must cope, compliance with international standards would impose an added variable to the decision calculus of the financial manager.

CONCLUSIONS REGARDING UNDERWRITERS, ACCOUNTING DIVERSITY, AND CAPITAL MARKET EFFECTS

Accounting diversity is regarded as a problem by seven out of eight underwriters in our sample. This is a problem, in turn, that is associated with capital market effects that range from the geographic scope of their underwriting activities to the pricing of international issues.

Our interpretation of these findings is that the responses of the underwriters reflect those of their clients. Underwriters are financial intermediaries that deal with corporate issuers from many countries. These issuers, in turn, adopt different financial disclosure policies based on the trade-offs we modeled with respect to financial and competitive costs. Given their financial disclosure decisions, some firms will be excluded from issuing in certain markets or face unfavorable financial terms. For these corporations, the effect on geographic location for raising long-term capital represents an ongoing cost.

Underwriters also deal with a heterogeneous investor clientele. A segment of this client population will be made up of MPCers; another segment will not. Based on our interviews with investors, we know that many of the non-MPCers are troubled by accounting diversity. These investors' reactions to accounting diversity are very likely reflected in the comments we heard from underwriters.

Given the nature of their business, that is, serving as an intermediary between borrower and lender, underwriters must adapt to the decision needs of their clientele. For investors who are non-MPCers, restatement of foreign accounting numbers to a set of principles that are more meaningful to potential investors is a legitimate service activity. For the MPC segment of its clientele, specific advice on local accounting, financial, and cultural norms is an important service to provide. As one respondent remarked:

> If your clients want to have restated accounting numbers, you give it to them, regardless of how they use the information. Picking an attractive foreign stock can be likened to a beauty contest. In a beauty contest, what's important is not who *is* the most beautiful contestant. What's important is who the judges *think* is the most beautiful. Similarly, what's the most attractive stock, like beauty, lies in the eyes of the beholder. Whatever users feel is important is important. At the end of the day, what matters is what determines whether stock prices go up or down. Restated data is important in marketing securities to investors who are unfamiliar with foreign accounting methods or investments.

CONCLUSIONS REGARDING REGULATORS, ACCOUNTING DIVERSITY, AND CAPITAL MARKET EFFECTS

It appears that national regulators are not hindered by accounting diversity in making their regulatory decisions. All have adopted coping mechanisms that may reflect the historical structure of a country's regulatory environment, the relationship that each regulatory body has with its constituencies, and other capital market norms that are unique to each country.

Extremes in regulatory disclosure requirements can have adverse effects on the location of market activity and, therefore, market growth. Accordingly, the issue of identifying an optimum disclosure framework for international corporate issuers or listers is an important consideration among some regulators.

The demand for harmonized accounting standards does not seem to be emanating from most of the market regulators we surveyed. Many regulators seem to prefer alternatives to those being advanced by the International Accounting Standards Committee. Support for international accounting standards stems not so much from the adverse effects of accounting diversity on regulatory decision processes as it does from the competitive market for regulation, that is, the desire among regulators to find acceptable accounting principles and disclosure levels that, when adopted by all regulators, will not disadvantage one national capital market to any other in its competitive bid to attract foreign issuers or listers.

CONCLUSIONS REGARDING OTHER SURVEY RESPONSES, ACCOUNTING DIVERSITY, AND CAPITAL MARKET EFFECTS

Responses from the other users we sampled confirm our findings with respect to the investor group. Those who restate financial statements from one set of accounting principles to another report that their decisions are affected by accounting diversity. On the other hand, the decisions of those embracing local accounting norms (those whom we have labeled MPCers) are not affected by accounting diversity.

This suggests that users of accounting information face a choice problem—to restate from one accounting framework to another or to generate a facility for using and properly interpreting local accounting norms—with cost and benefits associated with each. Users of international accounting data appear to have done the decision calculus, and each has concluded that its posture is optimum.

CHAPTER 7

STUDY IMPLICATIONS

In this chapter, we expand on the conclusions of our study by describing some of the implications of international accounting diversity for capital market participants. Policy implications for regulators are complex. They are discussed separately in Chapter 8.

A major implication of our findings is that accounting differences *are* important and affect the capital market decisions of a significant number of market participants, regardless of nationality, size, experience, scope of international activity, and organization structure. Based on the responses we have received from active market participants, the presumption of international capital market efficiency is not a foregone conclusion.

INVESTORS

Organizational choices on how to approach the international market have a direct bearing on the nature of responses received from investors regarding the effects of accounting diversity on their capital market decisions. Virtually all of the institutional investors we spoke to follow some variation of a *top-down approach*—that is to say, asset allocation across countries on the basis of macroeconomic variables. The choices of countries may be tempered by parameters for market size, liquidity, absence of capital controls, political risk, and so forth. But portfolio weights are typically determined for countries rather than for industries. Given these allocations, investors are led to ask which stocks are the best *within* countries, rather than which are the best within an industry but *across* countries. As a result, comparative analysis of firms across countries (with differing accounting principles) is discouraged.[1]

The importance of the country factor was cited by one of the investors in our sample when it switched from being organized by industry to being organized by country.

> In the 1960s, our teams were organized by industries. And in 1971 we changed that and organized our research by market. The primary assignment remains "by country," because it's very seldom that, for example, pharmaceuticals around the world move together. Usually, they move up in Japan and down in Germany—not as a group, but rather because the Japanese market (for various reasons) is well positioned, and the flow of liquidity and cash into the market is strong. . . . There are some industries (basic raw materials, oil) which escape that, but there are very few industries.

While analysis of investments on a country-by-country basis minimizes the need for direct comparisons between similar firms in the same industry but headquartered in different countries, cross-country comparisons are necessarily made in large investment houses that have centralized committees for approvals of stock selections. By implication, these investors must have some mechanism, implicit or explicit, for making cross-country comparisons. However, many of the investors we spoke to warned that there is no universal standard of comparison.

> You look at all the ingredients that the Japanese market is looking at. For instance, we buy Japanese stocks at 60 times earnings. And you find our Japanese specialist will come to our morning meeting saying, "This stock has retreated to 45 times earnings. It's darned cheap and you've got to buy it." And then in the next five minutes, you will have the man following the Dutch stocks saying, "This stock is now over-priced at 9.5 times earnings." Because in the Netherlands 10 times earnings is today and has been historically expensive. The point is that there is no standard throughout time and throughout geographical areas.

---

[1]It is interesting to note that the theoretical literature in international investment has also developed along these same lines. Empirical studies using data from the 1960s and 1970s by Lessard (1976) confirm that the country factor is the most important single factor determining the worldwide variation in security returns. This was followed by an industry factor and then a common world factor.

Almost like travelling from meeting to meeting where English, French, or German is spoken, these investors argued that it was possible to conduct the meeting in any language without an effect on the outcome. By implication, those who needed a translation or a restatement might learn something, but they also might be misled.

The widespread use of the top-down, country allocation approach to international investing raises the question as to what extent this approach was influenced by the difficulties of dealing with international accounting diversity. Our findings suggest that, for many investors, accounting diversity is a barrier to cross-country comparisons. An implication for investors is that for this segment of the investing community, additional effort in improving accounting restatement algorithms or better application of existing algorithms may be worthwhile. As noted, however, in the absence of uniform valuation standards around the world, proper interpretation of restated numbers will depend on a thorough understanding of the company and the environmental context within which the restated numbers are generated. When using the restatement approach to selecting stocks within countries, investors should examine whether restatement affects the rank-ordering of firms. If the rank-ordering of investment opportunities is unaffected, then efforts to restate would appear superfluous. As an alternative coping strategy, investors may rely on variables that are less sensitive to accounting differences (e.g., discounted dividends, rates of change, macroeconomic variables, and the like).

Based on our survey, investors who make the effort to understand the firms in a foreign country on their own terms, that is, familiarize themselves with local environmental norms and develop skills in interpreting foreign accounts in their original form, are least likely to encounter problems caused by accounting differences. In taking this MPC approach, such expertise can be developed in-house or by relying on local talent.

ISSUERS

Accounting statements assist firms in measuring their performance and communicating these results to investors. One implication of our study is that firms face the choice of how much they wish to accommodate the information needs of investors and other readers of their accounting statements. In communicating with an investor population whose tolerance for accounting diversity varies, firms have several options from which to choose. They can opt to restate their reported numbers to the accounting framework of the reader's country-of-domicile. In doing so, firms must be careful to avoid losing something in the translation. Supplementary disclosures that enable investors to understand the company and its operating environment seem called for. Alternatively, issuers can provide investors with their original financial statements. The text and currency framework may be translated but strictly for the reader's convenience. To avoid the risk of misunderstanding by readers who are not familiar with the reporting firm's accounting procedures, periodic road shows in which management meets with analysts to resolve accounting and other questions may be useful. A third option is for issuers to actively court sophisticated investors who understand their companies and can deal with accounting differences. Issuers noted that foreign investors may be more skittish; during periods of extreme volatility, they will fly to quality, dumping foreign stocks in favor of domestic stocks. These extra costs of keeping small foreign investors happy and informed were driving some firms to favor long-term, committed shareholders. Given the size of institutional investors and the advances of modern communications, it is just as economic for sophisticated investors to visit issuers of quality securities as it is for issuers to travel to foreign markets.

When there is a true need to raise funds for foreign expansion, for a foreign acquisition, or to raise capital beyond the capabilities of the local market, then issuers are in wide agreement that a presence in the foreign capital market may be required. However, when these conditions are not present, many firms doubt the advantages of worldwide listings, which may fragment the market for shares (raising bid-ask spreads) and possibly add a cadre of nervous, short-term-oriented shareholders. Some firms admit that multiple foreign listings are primarily a marketing device (for consumer products) and that the real financial marketing of the firm takes place with professional analysts at headquarters.

Corporate issuers from the United States and, in some cases, the United Kingdom appear to have greater flexibility in accessing international capital markets than issuers from other countries in our sample. While this may be partially attributed to the asymmetry we observe between the United States and other national regulators with regard to accounting requirements, it appears that greater corporate transparency is an important ingredient in affording firms access to certain capital markets. This is especially applicable for less-large, non-U.S. firms whose international funding experience is limited. By the same token, however, the practice of accounting reciprocity on the part of regulators outside the United States affords U.S. issuers a wide range of geographic choices for their funding.

Corporate size, as well as nationality, has a bearing on funding flexibility. Large, well-known companies appear likely to have greater flexibility than less-large firms in terms of their capital market access. Accordingly, they do not have to cater as much to non-MPCers and are less concerned about accounting considerations.

We have repeatedly made the point that information entails both costs and benefits for firms and that firms may not release information to minimize their financial cost of capital if by doing so their competitive costs are increased. In various ways, we saw this view validated in our interviews. One issuer made our point very directly:

> Our annual report is not the most open. We have to draw the line between informing the investor (after all, we are investors ourselves) and what we provide to the competition. We tend to draw the line on a short basis. But then, we hold road shows.

In this regard, firms in industries whose accounting rules depart from GAAP and who feel that they are being examined by top-down investors should provide their accounts in conformity with industry norms to assure that they are being compared against the proper benchmark. Operationally, this may be accomplished by comparing oneself with competing firms, both domestic and foreign. And, while corporate issuers whose published accounts are tax-driven can expect continued demands for greater transparency of what their reported numbers would look like on an adjusted basis, demands for greater *tax transparency* are likely to be made of firms whose published accounts tend to be based on generally accepted accounting principles.

A final implication regarding issuers concerns how these firms gain the expertise to communicate with analysts from around the world. First, firms may attempt to compare themselves with competing firms, both foreign and domestic, within the same industry. The level of precision in these comparisons may not be accurate enough for investment analysis, but as one issuer put it:

> You don't have to be that precise for those comparisons. Absolute
> precision doesn't help you very much. Getting to the third decimal point
> is not going to make a difference in your views.

Moreover, many of the firms we interviewed are large multinational firms with operations in several if not dozens of countries. Their foreign subsidiaries file accounting statements in foreign GAAP for statutory purposes. In some cases, headquarters will consolidate those figures and make cross-subsidiary comparisons for performance evaluations. Large multinationals may gain experience with numerous other accounting standards that helps them both to compare themselves with competitors and to explain themselves to foreign investors.

> Bear in mind that we're already converting U.S. accounts to our [local]
> accounts for a large part of our business anyway. So we're bound to be
> familiar with it.

This positive correlation between length of international experience, frequency of exposure to international markets, and the propensity to view accounting diversity as irrelevant highlights the channels through which diversity may pose a barrier to entry into international markets. It also suggests that a key coping mechanism for issuers may simply be perseverance and selective accommodation of investor information needs. If the investor's optimal coping mechanism is to be an MPCer, then the issuer's best coping mechanism may be to help the investor to implement an MPC approach.

UNDERWRITERS

In keeping with the tenets of the "hog cycle" for information, underwriters are likely to enjoy higher returns for their advisory services in international, as opposed to national, markets. Moreover, as margins in servicing the large, well-known corporate names have narrowed considerably, opportunities for charging genuine fees will lie in accommodating the needs of second- and third-tier firms.

As underwriters serve as intermediaries, courting issuers and selling their debt and equity issues to investors around the world, they can anticipate higher costs in taking non-U.S. clients to markets when their accounting does not conform with market standards. This again is likely to apply more to smaller issuers. Given the generalized cost of capital formulation described earlier in this study, underwriters need to maintain flexibility in taking their clients to alternate markets if conformity to regulatory or investor requirements in one country proves too costly. On the other side of the coin, accommodating the information needs of both non-MPCers and MPCers will prove a continued source of income.

As in domestic markets, international capital market participants are becoming more sophisticated. As a result, they are better able to judge the deals that are presented to them by underwriters. If their advice is judged to provide little in the way of added value, clients are likely to bypass them in favor of direct relationships with primary suppliers of funds and financial instruments. One issuer in seeking advice on a multiple listing put it quite bluntly:

> There's another factor that we have identified, and that is that there's an enormous fee . . . that is the driving force for underwriters. What we are doing, by-passing the underwriters, is costly in terms of our own time, but the fact is that we're trying to reduce the risk of volatility by having our shares in the retail [ADR] market. We are actually . . . identifying people whom we think are appropriate investors. Our pension managers have indicated to us, whether a firm does or does not have an ADR is totally irrelevant. Whether a firm is reporting its financial results according to one GAAP or another is equally totally irrelevant. They know the differences, they can make the adjustments. . . . We are saying that [for us] we don't see any evidence so far of an attraction of being quoted on all the world's major exchanges. The sort of people we would like to have as long-term investors in this company are perfectly well set up to buy and manage their shares in [our local market] if that's what they decide to do. It is our policy to make ourselves available directly to the top investors.

By the same token, however, when valid reasons exist, firms remain interested in foreign listings or offerings. For example:

> I think the best example of a justifiable, successful operation was at Ericson, which as you know was a small Swedish telephone exchange manufacturer. It developed this business very successfully and . . . it's had a huge explosion of its business. It became a major supplier of exchanges almost overnight. They introduced shares into the United States, and I personally feel that it was the logical thing to do.

A final question is whether regulatory changes (such as the U.S. SEC's Rule 144A[2] or harmonization of rules pertaining to new offerings) will affect the relationship between underwriters and institutional investors. While Rule 144A intends to expand the the ability of foreign firms to place securities in the United States, most large investors already have the freedom and mechanisms in place to invest in foreign securities already on foreign stock exchanges. To the extent that investors have already scanned the world for new investment opportunities, it may be that this particular rule change does little to enhance the currently growing appetite of Americans for foreign securities.[3] Other forms of institutional changes (such as harmonized and more efficient clearing and settlement procedures) would make international financial markets more attractive to foreign investors.

REGULATORS

In specifying appropriate reporting requirements for foreign issuers/listers, market regulators face a dilemma. Requirements that are too stringent discourage firms from issuing/listing their shares in that market. On the other hand, requirements that are too lenient discourage international investors from participating in such markets. At the same time, as investors gain in sophistication and learn to deal with accounting diversity, they can tolerate lower disclosure requirements. Under these conditions, mandated uniformity may minimize the ability of capital market participants to cope with change. What seems called for is reciprocity above some minimum threshold. Based on comments we have heard during our interviews, U. S. financial reporting and disclosure norms do not necessarily constitute the ideal threshold. Alternative frameworks include standards formulated by the IASC, the EC, or more likely some

---

[2]Essentially, Rule 144A exempts resale to large institutional investors from the registration requirements for the distribution of publicly offered securities under the Securities Act of 1933.

[3]Gurwitz (1989) argues that the development of the "144A market" may proceed slowly because various barriers and impediments will remain. For example, two likely participant groups—insurance companies and public employee pension funds—may face significant restrictions on the volume of foreign securities they are permitted to buy. In addition, convenient trading, delivery and custodial mechanisms will need to evolve along with standards for documentation and disclosure under Rule 144A.

market-determined standard. Possible scenarios, together with their benefit/cost tradeoffs are discussed in Chapter 8.

At present, non-U.S. firms appear to be bearing more of the costs associated with accounting diversity. Based on our interviews, many non-U.S. issuers would immediately come to the U.S. market if the SEC's disclosure requirements were modified. The evolution of the "144A market" will provide an important test case. Market regulators in the United States can expect heightened lobbying efforts from this audience-of-interest.

In formulating a set of reporting requirements for foreign issuers/listers, market regulators should not separate disclosure issues from accounting measurement issues. If companies are requested to provide additional disclosures but are provided leeway in measuring what is disclosed, the resulting information will be judged unreliable. Accounting measurements and disclosure are closely intertwined.

CHAPTER 8

POLICY RECOMMENDATIONS

In this study, which examines an issue at the intersection of international accounting and international capital markets, we have drawn upon several important themes.

First, a fundamental tenet of accounting is that the accounting measurements for a firm should present an accurate reflection of the underlying economics of that firm. Since macroeconomic conditions, tax policies, regulatory policies, managerial incentives, cultural factors, and so forth vary across countries, there is reason to expect that accounting conventions will vary from situation to situation.

Second, corporate financial theory predicts that while companies have incentives to provide information to investors in order to reduce their cost of funds, companies also have an incentive to restrict disclosure of information in order to reduce their competitive costs. In this framework, the desire of companies to select the optimal amount and type of information preparation and disclosure is easily understood. Recalling again the degree of diversity in the world (e.g., macroeconomic, tax, regulatory, cultural), it would be sheer coincidence if the optimal amount and type of information were the same for every firm. In fact, we have noted the examples of private markets (i.e., the Euromarkets) and private regulators (i.e., the London Stock Exchange), where companies have tailored their information provision (either more or less) to suit market conditions.

Finally, we have noted the tremendous level of activity in international capital markets and its growth over the last decade. While accounting diversity may be a deterrent to some individuals and firms, many of the institutions we surveyed have worked to develop what they feel are effective coping mechanisms. Some investors adopt the MPC approach and employ specialists in national security analysis, including national accounting practices. Some issuers provide restated information or additional disclosures, while others hold fast to their domestic accounting principles and enter the Euromarkets. Some regulators accommodate diversity by developing the skills to assess foreign companies, or they rely upon sponsoring banks to share in the liability. Other regulators simply do not subscribe to the notion that a government regulator must protect domestic investors from the risks of investing in foreign firms.

Nevertheless, while the international financial markets have worked, and in many senses have prospered, this performance begs the question of whether some other accounting system—one that reduces the amount of diversity that now exists—would serve the international community still better. As we stress in Chapter 1, the question of the optimal degree of international accounting harmony is a complex empirical matter. For reasons reviewed in Chapter 1 and highlighted above, simple nominal accounting harmony (everyone using the same accounting principles everywhere, but harmony in name only) need not produce more meaningful and useful accounting reports. To repeat a testimonial cited earlier:

> . . . there is a danger that international standards delude the unsophisticated into thinking that you've genuinely harmonized. It may in fact be healthy to have things look a little different because it makes people realize that there are some differences.

When a reader wishes to perform a comparative analysis on two firms from different countries, it is useful to decompose observed accounting differences into three sources: (*a*) accounting rule differences, (*b*) environmental differences, and (*c*) real differences in those attributes being measured. At present, when a reader wishes to compare several automobile companies (e.g., Fiat, Toyota, and Chrysler) or several electrical companies (e.g., Philips, Hitachi, and General Electric), it is true that accounting rule differences may inject a barrier to the analysis. For the sake of analysis, suppose accounting rules were harmonized. Would it follow that the reader's difficulties with comparative analysis would be solved or at least simplified? The answer is *No*. First, it is clear that factor (*b*) representing national macroeconomic, tax, regulatory, and cultural differences would still remain. Readers would have to understand these factors in order to accurately assess the condition of each firm. Second, and more important, if firms were being regulated, taxed, or managed on the basis of accounting figures *not* identical with the reported harmonized figures, then readers would have to take the reported accounting figures and rework them to arrive at more meaningful numbers. This is simply the case of a harmonized accounting convention treating *un*like things as if they were alike.

Our primary conclusion in the policy area is that policy prescriptions regarding international accounting must be based on empirical evidence. We revert to the paradigm that accounting rules should be consistent with environmental norms—economic, cultural, and institutional. Following this principle, national accounting rules would be similar only to the extent that environmental systems (including tax policy, fiscal policy, regulatory objectives, managerial systems, performance incentives, and other cultural factors) were broadly similar across countries. The new supervisory guidelines for banking from the Bank for International Settlements, noted in Chapter 1, are a good illustration of this principle. Now that policymakers have agreed to uniform guidelines for bank supervision (including capital adequacy measures, risk rating measures, etc.) uniform accounting seems to be appropriate. The diversity in the manufacturing and service corporate sectors as seen against the backdrop of diverse economic systems poses the question of whether the necessary conditions are in place to recommend a uniform international accounting system. Logically, accounting harmony *follows* from (what we have called) economic and cultural harmony, not the reverse.

The observation that accounting diversity represents a cost to society is *not* by itself sufficient to recommend a change in the status quo. A policy recommendation to alter the status quo presumes that the impact of a new policy can be predicted and that the benefits of a new policy outweigh the costs of imposing it. Several policy alternatives are available to deal with the concerns of various constituencies regarding accounting diversity. It is useful to think of the policy choices as representing tradeoffs between costs (disadvantages) and benefits (advantages).

In the remainder of this chapter, we outline four generic policy alternatives.[1] For each alternative, we discuss the perceived benefits and

---

[1]These generic policy alternatives do not preclude hybrid options based on combinations of the four basic themes. For example, firms might supplement financial statements prepared for parent-country readers (*primary* statements) with financial statements prepared according to international accounting standards (*secondary* statements). Another alternative is international standards that specify a *preferred* treatment, where permitted alternatives are reconciled to the preferred treatment.

costs, in some cases drawing on our interview findings or remarks made during the interviews. Our interviews have revealed that accounting issues are an important problem for large and small investors analyzing small firms from small, developing countries. This was not viewed as a problem of accounting diversity but, rather, of transparent and credible accounting standards and systems of *any* sort. There is no question that small firms from small countries would benefit by a general improvement in accounting practices and disclosure, according to *any* system of accounting and auditing practices. The policy debate that we are addressing really applies more to firms from large countries with well-developed traditions of accounting and auditing systems in place.

HARMONIZATION OF NATIONAL ACCOUNTING PRINCIPLES

Perceived Benefits

The primary perceived benefit of harmonization is that by standardization of accounting rules, financial analysis of firms would be simplified. Rather than learning a myriad of accounting conventions in numerous countries, an analyst need learn only one. A single international accounting language would link the world—analogous to Esperanto, the artificial international language designed to make national languages obsolete. Harmonization would increase the number of readers qualified to examine accounting statements from foreign countries. And it might increase the confidence that people had in their understanding of foreign companies. This in turn would encourage international investing and issuing activities. These capital flows would increase capital market efficiency, providing benefits to both investors and issuers in the markets.

Perceived Costs

To begin, an expressed desire for harmonization simply raises the question of what form of harmonization is to be selected. Harmonization to one standard will impose different costs and benefits on different parties than would harmonization to another. If the presumption is that a new international accounting standard will reflect a change in principles or a change in disclosure for at least some countries, then clearly firms from these countries will incur extra preparation costs and extra competitive costs that they do not now incur. Harmonization also raises the issue of whether a new standard would be completely rigid or whether choices would be permitted. If the allowed choices are many, then whatever gains might come from reducing accounting diversity will be few.

The largest perceived cost of harmonization stems from the concern that the standardized accounting rules will be out of synchronization with the underlying environmental conditions facing the firm and its managers. How will a harmonized standard be applied in countries that do not distinguish *tax* versus *external* reporting? Will managers optimize their harmonized figure or other tax, regulatory, or managerial accounting figures? If managers do not optimize their harmonized figures, will the new figures be more revealing to readers? Or will it simply be a case of making unlike things appear like, thus confusing or misleading readers?

Harmonization also entails certain political costs. Countries may lose part of their sovereignty if their fiscal tax base is based on externally imposed harmonized accounting numbers. Companies would also lose the flexibility to supply different or less information and source their external finance through the Euromarkets. Companies would bear the preparation costs of new standards and the competitive costs of additional disclosures. They would not necessarily gain through a lower cost of external funding.

RECIPROCITY

Perceived Benefits

Reciprocity implies that national regulators would accept the accounting statements of foreign companies as prepared. Decisions to allow an underwriting or a listing would be made on the merits of each case.

There are several advantages to a system based on reciprocity. First, there would be no need for companies to change their current accounting procedures. Companies would incur no costs of change and no competitive costs from additional disclosures. Second, the accumulated experience of analysts in interpreting national accounting statements retains its value. There would be no need to retrain analysts to understand yet another accounting system, that is, international standards. Third, a system of reciprocity acknowledges national sovereignty and national economic and tax differences. Reciprocity would encourage the further opening up of capital markets.

Perceived Costs

The costs of reciprocity would fall primarily on those countries whose regulatory and accounting conventions were most at variance with other nations. The United States is perhaps the best example. Foreign accounting practices and disclosure policies would not satisfy current U.S. regulations for public offerings or listed securities. In this sense, U.S. issuers or listers would be held to a higher standard than non-U.S. issuers. This, in turn, could place U.S. issuers at a competitive disadvantage to issuers who are less forthcoming.

At present, the SEC does not judge the merits of any public offering or listing. The SEC's procedure is to check that all the relevant information is provided to investors. No liability is assumed for losses or mistakes made by the investing public. It is a buyer-beware system based on the assumption that the investing public has been supplied with all the *required* information in a largely standardized format and a common (accounting) language.

A system of reciprocity would force the SEC to either (*a*) analyze each application and approve them on their merits, or (*b*) pass along the onus of reviewing foreign company statements to the investing public. Strategy (*a*) would not be costless, since the SEC may not now have the expertise to judge foreign company applications for public offerings or listing on their own merits. In the United States, where the degree of share ownership by individuals is nontrivial, strategy (*b*) may be more costly. This may explain why the SEC has approved Rule 144A to allow foreign companies to offer securities for sale to large, institutional investors (defined as $100 million and above) rather than to the general public.[2]

In passing the costs of learning foreign accounting practices on to investors and underwriters, a system embracing reciprocity would undoubtedly result in costly errors for some investors. The uncertainty created by these errors and the lack of expertise might continue to

---

[2]Under Rule 144A, large institutional investors are presumed to have the competence to judge foreign investments based on foreign GAAP and varying levels of disclosure.

inhibit some investors and issuers from venturing into international markets.

HEIGHTENED DISCLOSURE

Perceived Benefits

In several interviews with institutional investors and underwriters, we heard the claim that if it is known *how* accounting numbers are constructed, then the analyst can figure out their economic meaning. In other words, principles differences were not viewed as a source of problems as much as disclosure differences. Professional analysts can deal with diversity, but they cannot easily cope with numbers that are hidden from view; in these cases they usually rely on estimates using indirect techniques.[3] Greater information availability and greater transparency, it can be argued, would improve investment decision making. This would in turn promote the further opening up of international capital markets.

Perceived Costs

The primary disadvantage of this policy alternative is that it imposes competitive costs on firms that are satisfied with their current levels of disclosure. Firms presently have the alternative of conducting road shows, in-house visits with analysts, private placements, or placements in the Euromarket. By their revealed preferences, many firms appear to find these alternatives satisfactory.

   While heightened disclosure might be sufficient for professional analysts, others might continue to have difficulty in comprehending the economic meaning of foreign financial statements. For example, small investors in the United States might be at a disadvantage in reading foreign statements, and for that reason the SEC might continue to re-

---

[3]Analysts may be able to assess the market value of certain assets (e.g., plant and equipment) by looking at their insurance values. More reliable measures of firm performance may be estimated from industry-wide trends on capacity utilization, employment, borrowings, etc.

strict public offerings of foreign companies that do not provide full U.S. GAAP disclosures.

MULTIPLE PRINCIPLES CAPABILITY

Policymakers could decide to retain the present regulatory guidelines. In that case, our results suggest that the wider development of MPC could result in more efficient coping. However, there might be costs as well as benefits.

Perceived Benefits

The benefits of a multiple principles capability (MPC) approach are largely similar to those under a policy of reciprocity. There would be no need to change accounting procedures now in place. The accumulated experience of financial analysts would retain its value. National sovereignty and national economic and cultural differences would be acknowledged. To the extent that underlying economic conditions vary from country to country, the MPC approach allows countries to tailor their accounting rules to the idiosyncrasies of their own economy. As more analysts understand the accounting rules and underlying economics of each country, confidence in international investing and issuing should increase, helping to further open up these capital markets.

Perceived Costs

Again, the costs of the MPC approach would be similar to those under a reciprocity approach. The MPC approach, however, does not address the question of whether foreign accounting practices satisfy domestic security market regulators. The United States stands out as a country that employs a national treatment policy. The SEC maintains a level playing field by opening up the U.S. capital market to all who supply U.S. GAAP statements and conform with other conditions. Its accounting and reporting requirements are applied uniformly to U.S. as well as foreign firms.

The MPC approach passes costs and risks back onto investors and analysts. If these costs are high and MPC learning is slow, international capital markets (and in particular the U.S. market) may not open up to the desired degree, thereby limiting the set of financial instruments that would otherwise be available to resident investors.

SUMMARY

Our brief overview of the costs and benefits of alternative policy proposals pertaining to international accounting rules should suggest that there is no easy answer. A well thought through proposal should be backed by empirical evidence. In the chapter that follows and concludes this report, we suggest some of the kinds of studies that would be useful to further policy discussions.

CHAPTER 9

SUGGESTIONS FOR FUTURE RESEARCH

Information plays a key role in the theory of finance. In the pricing of financial assets, investors set securities prices conditional on the available stock of information. Investors monitor security prices to detect and remove periods of inefficient pricing. Investors have incentives to collect additional information whenever the marginal return on information exceeds its cost. When information is costly to collect and analyze, investors will necessarily base their decisions on a subset of all possible information.

Issuers of securities also face decisions regarding information. As issuers provide more information about the firm, uncertainty is removed, which, ceteris paribus, will lower funding costs. Other factors, however, may not remain constant. The collection and processing of additional information often entails administrative costs. They may also entail competitive costs as other firms, labor unions, and industry regulators gain more knowledge about the firm. Additional information could lower the mean or raise the variance of expected profits for a particular firm, thereby raising its cost of funding.

Finally, securities markets regulators are concerned about the role of information. As watchdogs for investor protection, regulators will be tempted to maximize the amount and quality of information available to the public. Furthermore, it can be argued that the public will enjoy positive externalities associated with the provision of uniform categories of information that is comparable across firms. To maximize this positive externality, regulators prefer that standardized accounting principles and disclosure rules be applied to a broad range of firms. On the other hand, regulators have incentives to increase the amount of financial activity taking place within their regulatory domain. Excessive information requirements that raise costs to issuers without offering benefits to investors will lead to a migration of financial activity to markets that offer more favorable climates.[1]

Information—its availability, cost, and regulation—will help determine many of the key variables in financial markets, such as prices of individual securities, relative prices of comparable securities, and the volume and location of financial market activity. *Accounting information*, while an important element of this information set, is only one element. Information in the broadest sense—encompassing macroeconomic conditions, financial market conditions for settlement, liquidity, transaction costs, political considerations, cultural factors, and so forth—guides market participants in their investment, issuing, and regulatory decisions. As a result, it will be extremely difficult to determine the role played by accounting information, other factors holding constant.

Given that information at the level of the firm entails both costs and benefits, we would expect the optimum dimensions of information preparation and disclosure to vary from firm to firm. Both private and public policies reflect this notion. Private credit ratings agencies require a broad range of information beyond what is normally presented in a firm's public financial statements. In confidential meetings with ratings agencies, firms have a strong incentive to supply additional information. Similarly, regulators acknowledge that the balance between investor and issuer changes as one moves from private placements to public offerings of exchange listed securities to unlisted securities and so forth. Information requirements change accordingly. Issuers also recognize that there may be different segments of investors with different information requirements. The development of the Eurobond market is an illustration of a market that has developed without benefit of detailed regulations on information disclosure and investor protection.

Repeating our theme that the provision of information entails both costs and benefits, do issuers currently supply statement readers with an optimal measure of information in general and accounting information

---

[1]Migration of financial activity to enjoy a smaller net regulatory burden has been a common theme over the last 25 years. The development of the Eurocurrency and Eurobond markets are the classic examples. The development of London's SEAQ International Market for trading continental European equities is one of the more recent. See Levich (1990), Levich and Walter (1990), and Pagano and Roell (1990).

in particular? If too little or imprecise accounting information is generated, investor uncertainty will be high, raising the cost of funds. If too much accounting information is generated, firms will incur excessive administrative and preparation costs without any corresponding benefit.[2]

In the remainder of this chapter, we propose several empirical studies that would shed light on the market's response to international accounting differences. While not singling out an ideal world-wide accounting system, these studies would suggest the costs of the current system of accounting diversity and the ability of market participants to cope with it. We organize these suggestions according to whether they focus on investors, issuers, or the market as a whole.

INVESTORS AND INTERNATIONAL ACCOUNTING DIVERSITY

It is claimed, and many of those whom we interviewed agreed, that it is relatively more difficult to analyze foreign accounting statements. Those foreign investors who attempt to cope with accounting diversity must incur costs that domestic investors do not. It follows that local investors should earn higher returns from portfolio investment in their own markets than foreign investors earn in the same market. An analysis of institutional funds could test this proposition. One difficulty could be the practice of foreign firms compensating for their lack of knowledge by hiring local experts. If the local experts are available, then portfolio returns should be identical (on average) for funds managed by either local or foreign managers.

Similarly, credit evaluation is another task that may be more difficult across borders. The record of the major U.S. rating agencies for credit evaluation of both U.S. and foreign firms is open to evaluation. If credit evaluation of foreign firms is more difficult, we would expect to find more errors in classification of foreign firms than for domestic

---

[2]The provision of information into the public's hands may also have distributional effects. The value of insider information may be greater in a market (such as the United States) where it is known that the information will be made public and quickly reflected in prices. In other markets where certain information has been unavailable (say, consolidated income figures for Japanese companies), some analysts have said that this does not create a problem as the firms happily leak the information to large numbers of security analysts.

firms. Again, the use of local experts would lessen the possibility of misclassifications.

In our surveys with investors, we found that a small group of investors focused on the original accounting statements of the foreign firms (multiple principles capabilities) rather than performing a restatement. All investors using this MPC approach expressed satisfaction and the belief that their investment decisions were unaffected by international accounting diversity. An empirical study of the investment performance of MPC investors versus other groups might reveal whether the former do have better investment selectivity skills than the latter. It would also shed some light on the issue of whether or not accounting restatements have the potential to change the message of original numbers.

Alternatively, the decision utility of restated accounting numbers can be examined in terms of their ability to improve the measurement of investor decision variables. Specifically, are analysts' forecasts that are based on restated data more reliable than those based on original, unrestated data? Or is the converse the case? Do restated numbers change the rank-ordering of firms composing within-country portfolio selections?

At a more basic level, we do not know to what extent investor decision variables vary across national markets or whether there is increasing convergence. If security valuation models vary between markets and prices are driven by local decisions, efforts to assess whether accounting restatements provide relevant information may be premature.

In terms of corporate financial disclosure, there is room for studies that examine the extent to which institutional investors avoid diversifying into foreign countries whose accounting, disclosure, or auditing practices are judged to be inferior to domestic norms. Is there, for example, a correlation between country weights or required returns and the extent and comprehensiveness of corporate accounting disclosures? Do international investors place a value on higher audit quality, and how is that value manifested?

International mergers and acquisitions represent an area where precision in the valuation of foreign target assets is essential. Furthermore, in cases where a foreign acquisition results in a material change for the target firm, the acquiring firm may be required to present accounting statements (for the target firm and the proposed consolidated firm) to existing shareholders who are usually predominantly in the acquiring firm's country. The research issues in this area are, for example, whether foreign acquiring firms pay too much for target companies. In some cases the issue centers more squarely on accounting, as in the case of U.K. bidding firms that can write off goodwill immediately to reserves, while U.S. firms would be required to amortize goodwill, resulting in an ongoing charge to earnings.[3] Since numerous macroeconomic and strategic factors enter into M&A decisions, the role of accounting differences may be extremely difficult to isolate.[4]

ISSUERS AND INTERNATIONAL ACCOUNTING DIVERSITY

Issuers face the accounting rules and securities and tax regulations of their home country. To some extent, issuers have the flexibility to provide additional information over and above country minimums. This freedom is limited, especially in those countries that do not distinguish external financial reporting from tax accounting statements or accounting statements prepared for industry regulatory bodies. In the case where firms may produce only one set of accounting statements, any change in accounting practices for external purposes will have additional immediate cash flow effects via taxation or regulatory actions that must be costed out.

However, where they have the flexibility to alter their external reporting, firms should provide additional accounting information based

---

[3]The recent case of Blue Arrow, a U.K.-based firm with 65 percent U.S. ownership, offers an interesting illustration. Blue Arrow issues both U.S. and U.K. GAAP accounting statements. In January 1990, the company announced a writeoff of a huge portion of its deferred goodwill as a prelude to amortizing any remaining goodwill over a five year period rather than 40 years. The accounting charge resulted in an enormous impact on reported earnings. Share prices, however, were not affected by the announcement, suggesting that the underlying business fundamentals were unchanged. See Waller (1990).

[4]Empirical evidence in Tandon, Hassel, and Cakici (1990) suggests that foreign acquirers of U.S. targets have paid roughly the same bid premiums as domestic acquirers. However the results vary considerably comparing mergers versus sell-offs and comparing foreign acquirers across countries. In mergers, Japanese firms paid the highest bid premiums followed by Canadian firms. Merger bid premiums from U.K. firms were not significantly different than from non-U.K. firms. In cases of a sell-off of a U.S. business unit, German firms and U.K. firms paid significantly higher bid premiums than other foreign bidders. The study does not investigate whether accounting diversity was a significant factor in explaining these cross-country differences.

on a marginal cost versus marginal benefit calculation. Provision of additional accounting information should have a beneficial impact on the firm's cost of capital or price-earnings ratio, controlling for other factors.

An empirical test of this proposition could be carried out on a cross-sectional sample of data. Firms from a given country (say, France) have approached the international capital market with a variety of strategies:

Domestic (Paris) market listing only.

Unsponsored ADR shares trading over the counter.

Sponsored ADR shares, unlisted.

Sponsored ADR shares, exchange listed, full SEC disclosures.

Additional voluntary disclosures on London ISE.

After controlling for other factors, do these strategies affect the firm's cost of capital or its price-earnings ratio?

A similar study might be conducted on a time series basis by monitoring an individual firm over time and analyzing the impact of events such as listing or accounting information changes. Voluntary listing and accounting decisions ought to have a beneficial impact on the firm's shares. A problem with this approach is the possibility of a contagion effect. After the first firms, from say Denmark, propose an ADR listing, the market may anticipate that other firms will follow suit. If so, domestic share prices in Denmark and other near-by countries may move in advance of the actual accounting disclosure or listing changes.

Along similar lines, several firms in our sample have active investor relations programs. Do these investor relations activities have additional information content? Studies that measure abnormal returns during the period spanning company road shows seem warranted. In doing so, care must be taken to control for extraneous events that may have occurred during the same time period.

Our study suggests that differential disclosure requirements sometimes push corporate issuing or listing activities toward or away from certain capital markets. Do differential disclosure requirements explain some of the anomalies observed with regard to market size and extent of foreign listings cited in Table 1 of Chapter 2? Do foreign issuers in a highly regulated market such as the United States experience a higher cost of raising funds than that of a comparable U.S. counterpart, because of lower corporate transparency? Do corporate issuers switch auditors when raising funds in international capital markets, or is the market unaffected by differences in audit practices?

MARKET RESPONSES TO INTERNATIONAL ACCOUNTING DIVERSITY

In cases where foreign firms are listed on a U.S. exchange, they are required to prepare accounting statements consistent with U.S. GAAP in addition to their original accounting statements. However, there is typically a time lag between the release of the original accounting statements and those prepared according to U.S. GAAP. Does the release of the restated accounting figures provide additional information to the market? If share prices change after the release of restated, U.S. GAAP figures, then we can infer that the restated figures are valuable. If there is no share price change, then the restatement contains no new information. Preliminary evidence by Choi, Joo, and Kim suggests that, for a sample of Japanese firms, accounting numbers restated to a U.S. GAAP basis do not appear to possess information content.[5] The authors attribute this to the long time period between the release of original numbers and restated numbers filed with the SEC.

Exhibit 1 reveals great variations in price-to-earnings ratios across countries. Much more work is needed to explain why Japanese P/E multiples remain so much higher than similar ratios in Canada, Germany, Switzerland, the United States, and the United Kingdom, and to what extent these differences can be attributed to differences in accounting. In this case, researchers must control for company, industry, country, and international factors that could also affect P/E differentials.

At a more macro level, have accounting differences impeded the international flow of capital? Specifically, do we observe greater capital mobility between countries whose accounting and reporting practices are similar? Similarly, is there a correlation between differential national accounting, disclosure, and auditing standards and the relative volume of trading activity in various markets around the world?

---

[5]F. D. S. Choi, I. K. Joo, and Y. Kim, "The Information Content of Restated Accounting Numbers," unpublished paper, New York University, January 1990.

A major conclusion of this study is that it will be difficult to reach a consensus on uniform international accounting policies. Still, the notion of an optimal set of accounting measurement and disclosure rules continues to have theoretical appeal. At present some are advocating adoption of IASC standards as the proper norm. Others advocate harmonized standards along EC lines. Still others favor a policy of reciprocity.

While this debate is likely to continue, perhaps the markets will succeed where administrative efforts have failed. The Eurobond market with its distinctive features of international syndication techniques, flexible currency options, and relative freedom from rigid regulation has thrived. And London's SEAQ International has captured a large share of equity market trading by offering a flexible and efficient alternative to Continental European bourses. Perhaps those interested in accounting harmony would do well to look to these international markets for guidance.

TABLES

TABLE 1
Market Statistics on U.S., Japanese, and European Stock Exchanges (Values as of December 1988)

Country	Stock Exchange	Market Value of Domestic Firms (US $ millions)	Percent of Group Total	No. Listed Firms		Domestic Firms			
				Domestic	Foreign	Trading Volume (US $ millions)	Volume as % of Value	Value per Firm	Percentage Concentration 10 Largest Firms
Japan	Tokyo	3,814,800	42.3%	1,571	112	2,228,370	58.41%	2,428.26	18.6
U.S.	NYSE	2,413,900	26.8	1,604	77	1,356,000	56.17	1,504.93	15.2
	American	110,990	1.2	896	51[1]	31,170	28.08	123.87	N.A.
	NASDAQ	338,770	3.8	4,451	292[2]	347,080	102.47	76.09	N.A.
U.K.	London	734,200	8.2	1,993	587	475,043	64.70	368.38	25.4
Canada	Toronto	242,000	2.7	1,858	103	55,402	22.89	130.25	40.3
Germany	Frankfurt	229,770	2.5	609	474	349,214	151.98	377.29	46.6
France	Paris	222,290[3]	2.5	459	217	75,252	33.85	484.29	24.5
Australia	Sydney	181,210	2.0	1,393	36	38,192	21.08	130.09	24.7
Switzerland	Zurich	139,800	1.6	230	230	194,627	139.22	607.83	50.1
Italy	Milan	135,400	1.5	211	0	31,711	23.42	641.71	45.7
Netherlands	Amsterdam	103,600	1.2	232	228	62,203	60.04	446.55	67.0
Sweden	Stockholm	100,120	1.1	142	9	18,760	18.74	700.14	26.4
Spain	Madrid	91,120	1.0	369	0	20,834	22.86	246.94	45.4
Belgium	Brussels	58,780	0.7	186	151	10,686	18.18	316.02	58.3
Finland	Helsinki	30,630	0.3	142	9	7,111	23.22	215.70	41.9
Denmark	Copenhagen	26,970	0.3	260	7	5,107	18.94	103.73	37.7
Norway	Oslo	15,830	0.2	126	6	4,839	30.57	123.67	51.6
New Zealand	NZSE	14,430	0.2	295	156	1,121	7.77	48.92	66.2
Austria	Vienna	8,860	0.1	125	51	1,965	22.18	70.88	50.0
Total		9,013,400							

[1]As of December 31, 1987.
[2]Includes 196 foreign securities and 96 ADR shares.
[3]Includes the Second Market.

Source: Goldman Sachs International Limited, Anatomy of World Markets (London: Goldman Sachs. 1989); National Association of Securities Dealers, Inc., 1989 NASDAQ Factbook (Washington, D.C.: NASDAQ, 1989).

TABLE 2 Market Organization and Structure

	United Kingdom	Germany	France	Netherlands	Italy	Belgium	United States	Japan	Switzerland
Main exchanges	London	Frankfurt	Paris	Amsterdam	Milan	Brussels	New York	Tokyo	Zurich
Other exchanges	None	Eight	Seven	None	Ten	Four	Four	Seven	Two
Organization									
Ownership	Private	Public	Public	Private	Public	Public	Private	Public	Private
Regulation	Self-regulated	Mostly self-regulated	Government	Self-regulated	Government	Government	Self-regulated and S.E.C.	Securities and Exchange Law	Government
Supervisory body	Council of the Stock Exchange	Borsenvorstand	Commission des Operations de Bourse	Control Commission	CONSOB[1]	Commission Bancaire	Board of Directors	Board of Governors	Association of Swiss Stock Exchanges
Is exchange monopoly?	Yes	No	Yes	Yes	No	Yes	No	No	No
Membership									
Brokers	Yes	Yes	Yes	Yes	Yes	Yes	Yes	Yes	Yes
Dealers	Yes (jobbers)	Yes (specialists)	No	Yes (specialists)	No	No	Yes	Yes	N.A.
Banks	No	Yes	No	Yes (limited)	No	No	No	Yes	Yes
Markets									
Spot market	Yes (limited)	Yes	Yes	Yes	Yes	Yes	Yes	Yes	Yes
Forward market	Yes	No (prohibited)	Yes	No	Yes	Yes	No	No	Yes
Settlement period	Biweekly	Two business days	Monthly (forward) Each session (cash)	Ten business days	Monthly	Biweekly (forward) Two days (cash)	Five business days	Four business days	Three business days
"Conditional" market	Yes	Yes	Yes	Yes	Yes	Yes	N.A.	N.A.	No

	Unlisted Securities Market (USM)								
"Second" market	—	Yes (since 01/83)	No	No	Yes (begins 01/85)	N.A.	N.A.	N.A.	N.A.
Orders									
Market orders	Yes	Yes	Yes	Yes	Yes	Yes	Yes	Yes	Yes
Limit orders	Yes	Yes	Yes	Yes	Yes	Yes	Yes	Yes	N.A.
Price determination									
Periodic call auctions	No	Yes	Yes	Yes	Yes	Yes	No	N.A.	N.A.
Continuous auction market	Yes (active stocks)	No	Yes (active stocks)	No	No	No	No	Yes	Yes
Primarily dealer market	Yes	No	No	No	No	No	No	N.A.	N.A.
Trading hours	9:00–16:00	9:30–11:00 12:30–14:30	9:30–11:00 12:30–14:30	10:00–16:30	10:00–13:45	11:30–14:30	9:30–16:00	9:00–11:00 (M–S) 13:30–15:00 (M–F)	10:30–13:15
Off-hour trading	Some	Yes	Some electronic trading	Some	Some	Very limited	No	No	Limited
Transaction costs									
Brokerage fee (range)	0.40–1.65%	0.75–1.10%	0.10–0.80%	0.70%	0.15–0.70%	0.75%	0.30–0.65%	0.15–1.20%	0.20–0.80%
Commission negotiable?	Not until 1986	No	No	No	No	No	Yes	No	No
Transfer taxes (range)	2% (with exceptions)	0.25%	0.15–0.30%	0.12%	0.06%	0.17–0.35%	No	0.01–0.30%	N.A.

¹Commissione Nazionale per la Società e la Borsa.

Source: Gabriel Hawawini, *Price Behavior and Efficiency*, New York University Monograph Series in Finance and Economics, no. 1984–4/5, 1984, pp. 26–29. Goldman Sachs International Limited, *Anatomy of World Markets* (London: Goldman Sachs, 1989).

TABLE 3
Listing Fees and Other Requirements on Major Stock Exchanges

	Number of Foreign Stocks Listed	Number of Foreign Stocks Listed during 1988	Form in which Foreign Stocks Traded	Initial Listing Fee[1]	Annual Listing Fee[1]	Necessary to Have Domestic: Sponsoring Bank?	Sponsoring Broker?	Market Makers?	Turnover Figures Available: Weekly?	Daily?	Settlement Period (working days)	Can Domestic Investing Institutions Buy Foreign Shares Not Listed on SE?	Are Foreign Listed Corporates Eligible for the Options Market?	Additional Accts. Required?	Periodic Reporting Required?
Sydney	50	9	All	A$2,586 ($1,200) upwards	A$415 ($190) upwards	No	Yes	n/a	Yes	Yes	5	Yes	Yes	Various	Semi-annual
Tokyo	112	26	Depository receipts	Y.2.5 million ($20,000) upwards	Y150,000 ($1,200)	No	Yes	n/a	Yes	No	4	Yes	n/a	Various	Semi-annual
Singapore	194[7]	—	All	S$2,000–S$20,000 ($1,040–$10,400)	S$400–S$20,000 ($208–10,400)	No	n/a	n/a	Yes	Yes	5	Yes	n/a	No	Semi-annual
Frankfurt	310	13	All	DM900–DM90,000 ($272–$27,256)	none	Yes	n/a	n/a	No[4]	No	2	Yes	Yes	No	Annual
Luxembourg	165	9	All	Lfr50,000 ($1,300)	Lfr20,000–Lfr100,000 ($520–$2,600)	No	Yes	1	No[5]	No[5]	5	Yes	Yes	No	Annual
Paris	205	16	All	none	none	No	Yes	n/a	Yes	Yes	1 month	Yes	Yes	Yes[6]	Annual

Amsterdam	297	7	All	Dfl16,000 ($3,000)	Dfl12,500– Dfl15,000 ($1,250– $2,500)	Either		n/a	Yes[5]	Yes[5]	10	Yes	Yes	No	Annual
London	538	33	All	£560– £35,710 ($990– $62,500)	£520– £9,320 ($910– $16,300)	No	Yes	2	Yes	Yes	–[2]	Most	Yes	IAS[3]	Semi-annual
Amex	51	5	Depository[8] receipts	$5,000– $30,000	$2,000– $30,000	Yes[8]	No	–[10]	Yes	Yes	5	Most	Yes	20F	Semi-annual
Nasdaq	273	14	Depository[8] receipts	$1,000	$250	Yes[8]	No	–[2]	Yes	Yes	5	Most	Yes	20F	Semi-annual
NYSE	80	12	Depository[8] receipts	$36,800 upwards	$14,630 upwards	Yes[8]	No	–[9]	Yes	Yes	5	Most	Yes	20F	Semi-annual
Toronto	67	6	All	C$3,500– C$25,000 ($1,680– 23,000)	C$2,400– C$11,500 ($2,200– 10,600)	No	No	Yes	No[4]	No	5	Most	Yes	No	Annual

[1]Depends on number of shares listed and traded.
[2]Home market settlement period used.
[3]International Accounting Standards.
[4]Monthly figures available.
[5]Available on request only.
[6]Negotiable.
[7]182 are Malaysian.
[8]Most foreign listed shares in the US (apart from the many Canadian ones) trade in American Depository Receipt form (ADR) and as such, require a depository bank.
[9]One specialist allocated.
[10]One specialist, at corporate's choice.

Source: *Euromoney Corporate Finance* no. 52 (March 1989, p. 40).

TABLE 4
Comparison of International Accounting Principles

Accounting Principles	UK	USA	France	Germany	Netherlands	Sweden	Switzerland	Japan
1. Consistency—accounting principles and methods are applied on the same basis from period to period	Yes	Yes	Yes	Yes	Yes	PP	PP	Yes
2. Realization—revenue is recognized when realization is reasonably assured	Yes	Yes	Yes	Yes	Yes	Yes	PP	Yes
3. Fair presentation of the financial statement is required	Yes	Yes	Yes	Yes	Yes	Yes	Yes	Yes
4. Historical cost convention—departures from the historical cost convention are disclosed	Yes	Yes	Yes	Yes	Yes	Yes	RF	Yes
5. Accounting policies—a change in accounting principles or methods without a change in circumstances is accounted for by a prior year adjustment	Yes	No	Yes	MP	RF	MP	MP	No
6. Fixed assets—revaluations—in historical cost statements, fixed assets are stated at an amount in excess of cost which is determined at irregular intervals	MP	No	Yes	No	RF	PP	No	No
7. Fixed assets—revaluations—when fixed assets are stated, in	Yes	No	Yes	No	Yes	Yes	No	No

historical cost statements, at an amount in excess of cost, depreciation based on the revaluation amount is charged to income

8. Goodwill amortized	MP	Yes	Yes	M	Yes	MP	Yes
9. Finance leases capitalized	Yes	Yes	No	No	No	RF	No
10. Short-term marketable securities at the lower of cost or market value	Yes	Yes	Yes	Yes	Yes	Yes	Yes
11. Inventory—valued at the lower of cost or market value	Yes	Yes	Yes	Yes	Yes	Yes	Yes
12. Manufacturing overhead allocated to year-end inventory	Yes	Yes	Yes	Yes	Yes	Yes	Yes
13. Inventory costed using FIFO	PP	M	M	M	PP	PP	M
14. Long-term debt includes maturities longer than one year	Yes	Yes	No[1]	Yes	Yes	Yes	Yes
15. Deferred tax recognized where accounting income and taxable income arise at different times	Yes	Yes[2]	No[3]	Yes	No	No	Yes
16. Total pension fund assets and liabilities excluded from a company's financial statements	Yes	Yes	No	Yes	Yes	Yes	Yes
17. Research and development expensed[4]	Yes	Yes	Yes	Yes	Yes	Yes	Yes
18. General purpose (purely discretionary) reserves allowed	No	Yes	Yes	Yes	Yes	Yes	Yes

TABLE 4—Continued

Accounting Principles	UK	USA	France	Germany	Netherlands	Sweden	Switzerland	Japan
19. Offsetting—assets and liabilities are offset against each other in the balance sheet only when a legal right of offset exists	Yes	Yes	Yes	Yes	Yes	Yes	PP	Yes
20. Unusual and extraordinary gains and losses are taken to the Income Statement	Yes	Yes	Yes	Yes	Yes	Yes	Yes	Yes
21. Closing rate method of foreign currency translation employed	Yes[5a]	Yes[5a]	Yes	Yes	Yes	No[5b]	Yes	No
22. Currency translation gains or losses arising from trading are reflected in current income	Yes	Yes	MP	MP	MP	MP	MP	No
23. Excess depreciation permitted	Yes	No	Yes	Yes	Yes	Yes	Yes	Yes
24. Basic statements reflect a historical cost valuation (no price level adjustments)	Yes	Yes	Yes	Yes	M	Yes	Yes	Yes
25. Supplementary inflation—adjusted financial statements adjusted	MP	MP	No	No	MP	Yes	No	No
26. Accounting for long-term investments:								
(a) less than 20% ownership—cost method	Yes	Yes	Yes	Yes	No[6]	Yes	Yes[7]	Yes
(b) 20–50% ownership—equity method	Yes	Yes	Yes[6]	No	Yes	MP	M	Yes

(c) More than 50% full consolidation	Yes	Yes	Yes[6]	Yes	Yes	Yes	Yes	Yes
27. Both domestic and foreign subsidiaries consolidated	Yes	Yes	Yes	M	Yes	Yes	MP	Yes
28. Acquisitions accounted for under the purchase cost method	PP	PP	Yes	Yes	Yes	PP	Yes	Yes
29. Minority interest excluded from consolidated income	Yes	Yes	Yes	Yes	Yes	Yes	Yes	Yes
30. Minority interest excluded from consolidated owners' equity	Yes	Yes	Yes	Yes	Yes	Yes	Yes	Yes

Key: PP—Predominant practice
MP—Minority practice
M—Mixed practice
RF—Rarely or not found
[1]Long-term debt includes maturities longer than four years.
[2]Deferred tax most commonly seen in conjunction with:
  1. *Provisions reglementees.*
  2. *Amortissement exceptionnel.*
  3. *Provisions pour payees congees.*
[3]Financial statements are orientated towards the tax calculations.
[4]To obtain the maximum benefit from tax allowances, the most favorable tax-orientated valuations have to be taken up in the financial statements.
[4]Under certain circumstances research and development expenses can be capitalized.
[5]a. In certain cases the temporal method is acceptable.
  b. Monetary/non-monetary method of foreign currency translation used.
[6]Proportional consolidation can also be used.
[7]Equity/net asset value method used.

Source: UBS Philips & Drew, *Understanding European Financial Statements* (Basel: Union Bank of Switzerland, June 1987), pp. 4–5.

TABLE 5

International Diversity in Auditing Practices (International Conformity with IAPC ED No. 12, in percent)

Country	N	Form of Report							
		Title given	Addresses identified	Auditor signed	Auditor's address	Report dated	Scope and opinion in separate paragraphs	Report indexed	Report's location (% by itself)
Far East and Asia:									
Australia	N=25	100	4	100	88	100	88	52	12[D]
India	N=20	100	5	100	95	100	100	85	80[A]
Japan	N=76	95	84	100	91	100	97	59	47[D]
Malaysia	N=20	100	0	100	95	100	100	90	70[D]
Philippines	N=9	100	67	100	100	100	89	67	67[Mixed]
Singapore	N=5	100	0	100	100	100	100	60	40[D]
Taiwan	N=7	86	57	71	73	85	100	29	43[D]
Thailand	N=6	88	88	100	87	100	100	13	100[A]
Americas:									
Brazil	N=6	50	50	100	100	100	100	50	67[D]
Canada	N=40	100	88	100	100	100	100	47	30[Mixed]
Mexico	N=7	71	71	100	100	100	71	0	100[D]
United States	N=125	98	87	100	100	100	81	55	14[D]
Europe:									
Austria	N=8	0	0	100	100	100	0	0	0[C]
Belgium	N=13	100	8	85	85	85	100	62	69[D]
Denmark	N=14	86	0	100	100	100	77	21	29[Mixed]
Finland	N=20	100	0	100	100	100	95	100	55[D]
France	N=46	100	4	98	83	95	96	63	57[A]
Germany	N=60	10	0	100	100	100	7	5	15[B]
Ireland	N=10	100	0	100	100	100	100	100	90[A]
Italy	N=8	75	50	50	25	37	44	37	100[A]
Netherlands	N=25	100	4	100	100	100	100	76	72[D]
Norway	N=10	90	20	100	90	100	100	80	10[D]
Spain	N=11	82	82	91	9	73	91	64	55[D]
Sweden	N=34	100	3	100	30	100	100	79	35[D]
Switzerland	N=19	95	21	100	19	100	100	79	90[D]
United Kingdom	N=60	100	0	100	57	100	97	95	50[A]
Africa:									
South Africa	N=10	100	0	100	80	90	70	80	10[A]

	Country		Scope				Opinion		
			Country's name	Financial statements identified	Date/Period covered	Reference to auditing standards	True and/or fair	Conformity	Consistently applied
Far East and Asia:	Australia	N=25	92	68	96	0	100	96	4
	India	N=20	95	30[E]	100	55	95	100	5
	Japan	N=76	100	100	100	100	100	99	96
	Malaysia	N=20	10	100	100	5	100	100	0
	Philippines	N=9	100	100	100	100	100	100	100
	Singapore	N=5	20	100	100	100	100	100	0
	Taiwan	N=7	100	86	100	86	86	86	86
	Thailand	N=8	100	100	100	100	100	100	100
Americas:	Brazil	N=6	100	100	100	100	100	100	83
	Canada	N=40	98	97	100	100	100	100	100
	Mexico	N=7	100	29[E]	100	86	86	100	86
	United States	N=125	99	100	100	100	100	100	100
Europe:	Austria	N=8	0	0[F]	0	88	0	100	0
	Belgium	N=13	46	46[EF]	100	77	39	100	15
	Denmark	N=14	57	36[E]	100	79	29	93	0
	Finland	N=20	95	0[F]	100	95	0	100	0
	France	N=46	52	71	100	65	22	76	35
	Germany	N=60	5	0[F]	4	93	2	100	2
	Ireland	N=10	50	100	100	40	0	100	0
	Italy	N=8	25	87	75	25	13	63	25
	Netherlands	N=25	100	20[F]	100	8	96	12	0
	Norway	N=10	90	0[E]	100	90	20	100	0
	Spain	N=11	91	27[EF]	100	18	0	64	18
	Sweden	N=34	24	3[F]	97	56	6	100	0
	Switzerland	N=19	37	42[E]	100	53	11	90	11
	United Kingdom	N=60	25	98	100	88	100	98	2
Africa:	South Africa	N=10	10	100	90	10	100	80	0

[A] Report located before financial statements
[B] In between financial statements
[C] After financial statements
[D] After financial statements and footnotes
[E] Uses the phrase "annual report"
[F] Uses the phrase "financial statements."

Source: F. D. S. Choi and G. G. Mueller, *International Accounting* (Englewood Cliffs, N.J.: Prentice Hall, 1984), pp. 347–48.

TABLE 6
Tests of Weak-Form Market Efficiency—A Sample from the French Market

Author(s) Year of Publication	Number of Shares or Indices Period of Analysis	Length and Definition of Returns	Statistical Tests Performed or Trading Rule Tested	Major Empirical Results	Conclusion
Semah/Serres/ Tessier (1970)	58 shares 1/64–2/69	Daily price changes (no adjustment for dividends).	Filter rules of variable size.	70% of shares beat buy-and-hold strategy after adjustment for transaction costs.	Reject the hypothesis that the market is weak-form efficient.
Solnik (1973)	65 shares 3/66–2/69	Daily, weekly, monthly percentage investment returns.	First order serial correlation coefficients.	Significant daily correlations (41/65) but none monthly (1/65). Correlation coefficient is stable.	Accept the RWM over monthly intervals.
Daloz (1973)	19 shares 21/10/68– 31/12/70	Price changes of 1, 2, 5, 10, and 20 days (up to 500 daily price observations).	Analysis of runs. Nonparametric tests. Serial correlation tests. Empirical frequency distributions.	Significant dependence over daily intervals but none over longer intervals. Distributions are leptokurtic.	Accept the RWM for intervals of 2 days or longer. Leptokutosis.
Hamon (1974)	28 shares 1/1/57– 31/12/71	Daily prices (adjusted for dividends).	Moving averages of size 25, 50, 100, 150, 200, and 250 days.	Optimal moving averages strategies beat a buy-and-hold strategy after deduction of transaction costs. But optimal.	Mixed. The market may be efficient but not perfect.

Galesne (1974)	99 shares 1/1/57–31/12/71	Daily price changes (adjusted for dividends).	Filter rules of variable sizes.	Filters seem to outperform buy-and-hold strategies even after deduction of transaction costs. However, the size of the optimal filter is not stable and in some cases filter strategies are too risky.	Accept the hypothesis that the market is weak-form efficient.
Hamon (1975)	102 shares 1/1/57–31/12/71	Daily price changes (adjusted for dividends).	Point-and-figure charts.	Significant daily dependence in price changes. Technical analysis, however, cannot outperform buy-and-hold strategy.	Accept the hypothesis that the market is weak-form efficient.
Hamon (1978)	131 shares 1/7/57–17/12/71	Daily log price ratios (adjusted for dividends).	Serial correlation coefficients of 1, 2, 3, 9, 10, 11, and 15 day lags.	78% of 1-day lag coefficients are significant and 68% of 11 day lag coefficient are significant.	Accept RWM over intervals longer than a day. It is not possible to take advantage of correlations to beat the market with either rules.
Bertoneche (1978)	76 shares 4/66–12/74	Daily, biweekly percentage investment returns.	First order serial correlation coefficients.	Significant daily correlations (41/65) but none monthly (1/65).	Reject the RWM over daily intervals. Accept over long intervals.

Source: Gabriel Hawawini, *European Equity Markets: Price Behavior and Efficiency*, New York University Monograph Series in Finance and Economics, no. 1984-4/5, 1984, pp. 36–53.

TABLE 7
Test of Semistrong Form Market Efficiency—Types of Studies by Country[1]

Type of Event Examined	Belgium	Finland	France[2]	Germany[3]	United Kingdom[4]	Japan[5]	Australia[6]	Singapore[7]	Hong Kong[8]
1. Stock splits/stock dividends and other changes in capitalization.	Brehain (1980)	Korhonen (1975c) Berglund-Liljeblom-Wahlroos (1985) Wahlroos-Berglund (1983)	Hamon	Schulz (1972)	Firth (1974)			Laurence (1986)	
2. Earnings/dividends announcements. Release of accounting numbers.	Fabry (1981) Ooghe-Beghin-Verbaere (1981) Beghin (1983) Brehain (1980)	Korhonen (1975e)	Giraud (1984) Hamon (1978) Outreville (1976)	Berndsen (1979) Brandi (1977) Coenen-berg-Brandi (1976) Moller (1982) Sahling (1981)	Firth (1976a) Cadle-Theo-bald (1981)	Jaffe-Westerfield (1985)			
3. New issues of common stocks/right offerings.		Berglund-Wahlroos (1985) Grandell (1983)	Jacquillat-McDonald-Rolfo (1978) McDonald-Jacquillat (1974) Vallot (1974)		March (1979)		Finn-Higham (1987)	Dawson (1987)	Dawson (1987)

4. Mergers and acquisitions.	Gagnon-Brehain-Broquet-Guerra (1982)	Husson (1984) Navatte (1978a,b)	Blaettchen (1981) (1982) (1983)	Firth (1976b) Franks-Broyles-Hocht (1977) Franks (1978)	Pettway-Yamada (1986) Hoshino (1982)
5. Changes in accounting rules and reporting methods.	Beghin (1983) Hawawini-Michel (1983) Hawawini-Michel (1981) Michel (1981)		Coenenberg-Schmidt-Werhand (1983) Coenenberg-Moller (1979)	Morris (1975) Standish-Ung (1982)	Pettway-Craig-Yamada (1988)

[1]These are the five countries for which more than one major study is available. Countries for which only one major study is available are Denmark (changes in capitalization), Italy (changes in dividend policy), and Sweden (earnings announcements). For details see Table 10 of Hawawini (1984).

[2]For France, Langohr and Vial et al (1983), (1984) have examined the reaction of the Paris Stock Exchange to the nationalization program of the Socialist government elected in May 1981.

[3]For Germany, another type of event examined is the announcement of changes in the organizational structure of firms [Buhner and Moller (1985)].

[4]For the U.K. there are other events whose effects on stock prices were investigated. Some of these are: (i) the published investment recommendations made in newspapers or furnished by advisory services [Firth (1972), (1975), (1978), and Dimson and Marsh (1984b)], the informational content of large investment holdings [Firth (1975)], the impact of changes in the money supply [Saunders and Woodward (1976)] and the ability of brokers to forecast stock returns [(Dimson and Marsh (1984a)].

[5]For Japan, other empirical studies have examined the dependence structure of share prices [Eun and Resnick (1988)], efficiency of the bond market [Kuroda (1982–1983)], the CAPM applied to the Tokyo Stock Exchange [Lau, Quay and Ramsey (1974)], and seasonality effects [Kato and Schallhein (1985)].

[6]For Australia, other empirical studies have examined weak-form efficiency tests [Praetz (1969)], the effect of traded options [Castagna and Matolcsy (1982, 1983)], the effect of inflation on security returns [Lamberton (1958)], and seasonality effects [Officer (1975)].

[7]For Singapore, other empirical studies have examined weak-form efficiency tests [Ang and Pohlman (1978), Hong (1978a, 1978b), D'Ambrosio (1980) and Laurence (1986)].

[8]For Hong Kong, other empirical studies have examined the weak-form efficiency test [Dawson (1981–1982, 1984)], and intervailing effects [Larson and Morse (1987)].

Source: References to research on European stock exchanges are from Hawawini (1984), pp. 18–19. See Hawawini (1984) for full bibliographic citations. References to research on Asian stock markets collected independently. Full citations are in the bibliography.

TABLE 8
The Market Value of U.S. and Japanese Equity Markets with and without Adjustments for Cross-Holdings, 1970–88

Year	Total Market Value (billions of dollars)		Adjusted Market Value (billions of dollars)		Fraction of Total World Equities	
	Japan	U.S.	Japan	U.S.	Japan	U.S.
1970	42.5	636.4	28.7	671.8	3.2	73.8
1971	67.2	741.8	43.7	784.7	4.0	72.1
1972	152.3	871.5	95.0	890.3	7.2	67.4
1973	128.6	721.0	83.2	668.2	7.8	62.9
1974	115.8	510.4	71.9	436.1	9.1	55.2
1975	135.1	683.6	84.9	660.8	7.7	59.8
1976	179.3	856.4	106.5	786.2	8.7	64.0
1977	205.1	793.9	125.6	742.1	10.0	59.1
1978	327.3	816.7	197.7	787.6	13.4	53.5
1979	274.0	960.2	167.5	923.5	9.9	54.6
1980	356.6	1240.0	214.6	1179.9	10.1	55.7
1981	402.7	1145.4	248.6	1106.7	12.2	54.3
1982	410.2	1308.3	235.1	1281.5	10.9	59.6
1983	519.2	1578.3	314.6	1506.3	12.2	58.3
1984	616.8	1593.2	368.4	1477.6	14.3	57.2
1985	909.1	1955.4	522.5	1845.7	14.7	52.1
1986	1746.2	2203.2	945.7	2187.2	19.6	45.3
1987	2978.2	2216.1	1382.5	2173.8	25.1	39.5
1988	3840.2	2480.9	1991.7	2397.1	29.5	35.5

Note: The total equity value for Japan is from Tokyo Stock Exchange, *Monthy Statistical Report*, and the value for the U.S. is from NYSE, NASDAQ, and SEC sources described in French and Poterba. The adjusted market values exclude intercorporate equity holdings.

Source: Kenneth French and James Poterba, "Are Japanese Stock Prices Too High?" manuscript, NBER Summer Institute, August 1989, p. 31.

TABLE 9

Gross Stock Transactions Involving the United States (Billions of U.S. Dollars)

A. Foreign Gross Purchases and Sales of U.S. Stocks by Country of Origin

Country	1982	1983	1984	1985	1986	1987	1988[1]
Japan	$ 2.0	$ 3.3	$ 2.7	$ 7.8	$ 26.9	$102.6	$120.6
United Kingdom	18.7	29.2	27.5	37.6	64.6	103.9	75.6
Canada	10.0	16.4	16.8	22.1	34.6	50.0	32.7
France	5.0	8.0	5.7	6.0	9.6	20.1	12.5
Germany	3.4	7.5	6.2	6.1	10.0	16.2	11.3
All Other	40.8	69.7	63.8	79.4	131.8	189.2	131.7
Total	$79.9	$134.1	$122.7	$159.0	$227.5	$482.0	$384.4

B. U.S. Gross Purchases and Sales of U.S. Stocks by Country

Country	1982	1983	1984	1985	1986	1987	1988[1]
Japan	$ 4.3	$ 8.0	$ 9.0	$ 11.6	$ 25.6	$ 47.7	$ 47.0
United Kingdom	3.6	6.5	7.8	13.3	32.6	67.8	46.7
Canada	2.9	5.0	4.4	6.8	9.8	18.8	11.8
France	0.8	1.3	1.0	1.2	4.2	6.1	3.5
Germany	0.5	1.2	0.9	1.9	6.1	8.6	4.8
All Other	3.6	8.3	7.6	10.9	21.9	40.4	27.9
Total	$15.7	$30.3	$30.7	$47.7	$100.2	$189.4	$141.7

[1]Preliminary 6-months data at annual rates, not seasonally adjusted.

Source: U.S. Government Accounting Office, *International Finance: Regulation of International Securities Markets* (Washington, D.C.: GAO, 1989), pp. 9–10.

TABLE 10
Twenty-Three Coded Items from Each Interview

A. Descriptive
   1. Country
   2. User group
   3. Size
   4. Scope of international operations
   5. Organization structure
   6. Length of international financial experience

B. Definition of accounting diversity
   7. Is it principles?
   8. Is it disclosure?
   9. Is it auditing?

C. Are your measurements hindered by diversity
   10. In GAAP?
   11. In disclosure?
   12. In auditing?

D. Does accounting diversity
   13. Affect your capital market decisions?

E. Do you cope with diversity
   14. In GAAP?
   15. In disclosure?
   16. In auditing?

F. Are there capital market impacts relating to
   17. Geography?
   18. Security types?
   19. Company types?
   20. Processing, information costs?
   21. Security valuation?

G. Regarding the future
   22. Do you plan to become more active in international financial markets?
   23. Do you favor harmonizing international accounting standards along the lines proposed by the IASC?

TABLE 11
Summary Findings for Investors, Issuers, Underwriters, Regulators, and Others

	Key Question: Does accounting diversity affect your capital market decisions?			
	Yes	No	N.A.	Total
Investors	9	7	1	17
Issuers	6	9		15
Underwriters	7	1		8
Regulators	0	8		8
Raters and others	2	1		3
Total	24	26	1	51¹

¹The International Accounting Standards Committee was interviewed but their answers are not included here.

TABLE 12

Summary Findings by Country, Size, Experience, Scope of Activity, and Organizational Structure

	Key Question: Does accounting diversity affect your capital market decisions?			
Country	*Yes*	*No*	*N.A.*	*Total*
U.S.	6	9		15
Germany	4	2		6
Japan	6	5		11
Switzerland	3	5		8
U.K.	5	5	1	11
Total	24	26	1	51
Size	*Yes*	*No*	*N.A.*	*Total*
Large	15	12		27
Less large	9	6	1	16
N.A.	0	8		8
Total	24	26	1	51
Experience	*Yes*	*No*	*N.A.*	*Total*
Long	14	18		32
Short	9	8	1	18
N.A.	1			1
Total	24	26	1	51
Scope of Activity	*Yes*	*No*	*N.A.*	*Total*
Limited	9	12	1	22
Extensive	15	14		29
Total	24	26	1	51
Organizational Structure	*Yes*	*No*	*N.A.*	*Total*
Centralized	13	15		28
Decentralized	10	11	1	22
N.A.	1			1
Total	24	26	1	51

TABLE 13
Capital Market Effects of Accounting Diversity: Investors

	From GAAP Differences	From Disclosure Differences
Geographic spread of investments	3	3
Types of companies/securities selected	6	7
Information processing costs	5*	2†
Assessment of security returns or valuation	8	8

*Two reported these costs were significant.
†Both feel this cost is significant.

TABLE 14
Issuer Characteristics (Size, Experience, and Scope of Operations) and Affect on Decisions

		Firm Size		
		Less Large	Large	
Affect on Decisions	Yes	4	2[b]	6
	No	2[a]	7	9
		6	9	15

[a]Two less large U.S. firms.
[b]One large Japanese and one large German firm.

		Experience		
		Short	Long	
Affect on Decisions	Yes	3	3[d]	6
	No	1[c]	8	9
		4	11	15

[c]One large, cash-rich firm with short experience.
[d]One Japanese and two German firms.

		Scope		
		Limited	Extensive	
Affect on Decisions	Yes	4	2[f]	6
	No	3[e]	6	9
		7	8	15

[e]Three firms that have accessed few markets, but including the United States.
[f]Two Japanese firms that have made extensive access of the Eurobond markets and non-U.S. equity listings.

TABLE 15
Capital Market Effects of Accounting Diversity: Issuers

	From GAAP Differences	From Disclosure Differences
Geographic location of funding/listing activity	3	6
Types of securities issued/investors courted	3	1
Information processing costs	5*	4*
Issuing costs/share valuation	7	3

*Three reported these costs were significant.

TABLE 16
Capital Market Effects of Accounting Diversity: Underwriters

	From GAAP Differences	From Disclosure Differences
Geographic spread of underwriting activities	3	7
Types of companies/securities selected	2	5
Information processing costs	6*	5*
Assessment of security returns or valuation	4	2

*Five respondents say this cost is significant.

EXHIBITS

EXHIBIT 1
Price/Earnings Ratio by Country

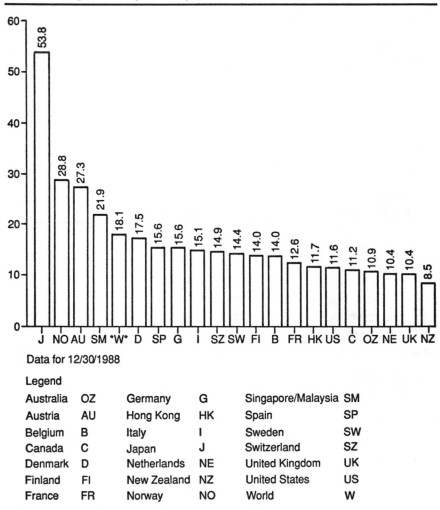

Data for 12/30/1988

Legend

Australia	OZ	Germany	G	Singapore/Malaysia	SM
Austria	AU	Hong Kong	HK	Spain	SP
Belgium	B	Italy	I	Sweden	SW
Canada	C	Japan	J	Switzerland	SZ
Denmark	D	Netherlands	NE	United Kingdom	UK
Finland	FI	New Zealand	NZ	United States	US
France	FR	Norway	NO	World	W

Source: Capital International.

EXHIBIT 2
Price/Cash Earnings Ratio by Country

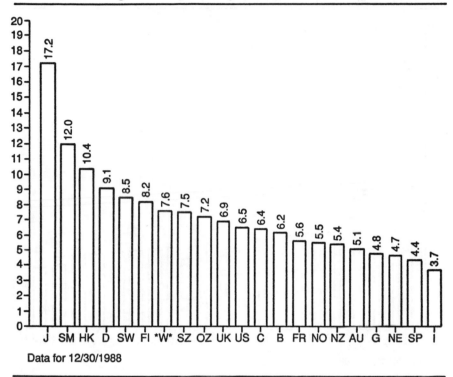

Data for 12/30/1988

Source: Capital International.

EXHIBIT 3
Price/Book Value Ratio by Country

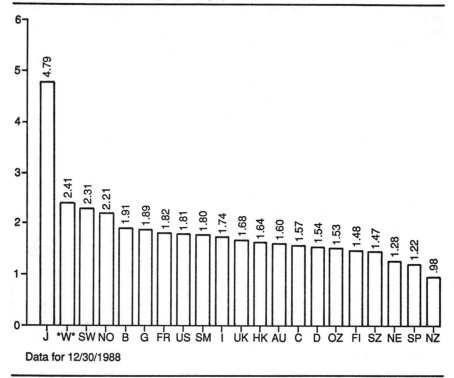

Data for 12/30/1988

Source: Capital International.

EXHIBIT 4
**Stock Price Performance and Accounting Earnings Announcements,
United States**

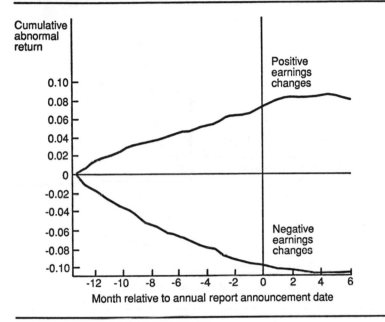

Source: R. Ball and P. Brown, "An Empirical Evaluation of Accounting Income Numbers," *Journal of Accounting Research*, Autumn 1968, p. 163.

EXHIBIT 5
**Stock Price Performance and Accounting Earnings Announcements,
Australia**

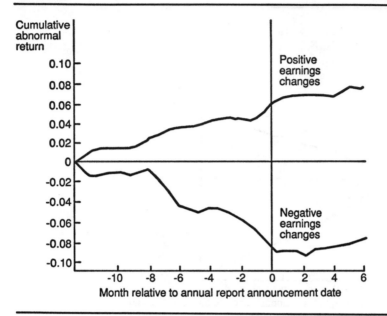

Source: Brown, "The Impact of the Annual Net Profit on the Stock Market," *The Australian Accountant*
40 (July 1970), p. 280.

EXHIBIT 6
Stock Price Performance and Changes in Accounting Techniques

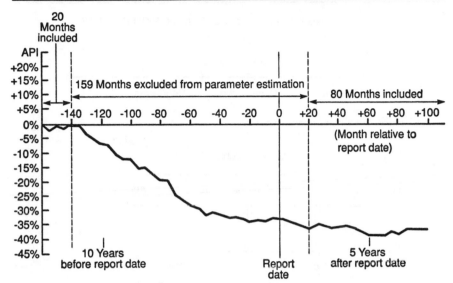

Abnormal performance for 197 firms making 267 accounting changes (including changes in depreciation policy, inventory methods, consolidation policy, accounting for investments and method of taking revenue into account) between 1947 and 1961.

Source: R. Ball, "Changes in Accounting Techniques and Stock Prices," *Empirical Research in Accounting, Selected Studies, 1972* (supplement), *Journal of Accounting Research* 10 (Spring 1972), p. 14.

EXHIBIT 7
Methodology and Survey Design

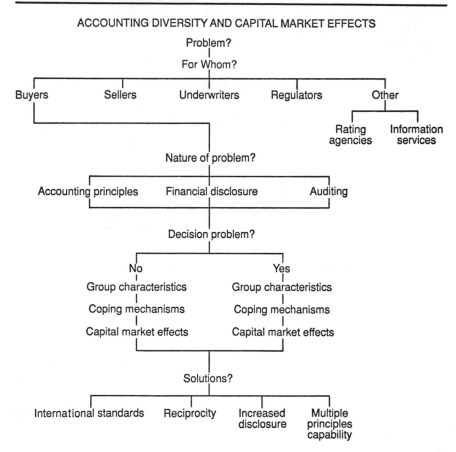

ACCOUNTING DIVERSITY AND CAPITAL MARKET EFFECTS

Problem?

For Whom?

Buyers   Sellers   Underwriters   Regulators   Other

Rating   Information
agencies   services

Nature of problem?

Accounting principles   Financial disclosure   Auditing

Decision problem?

No   Yes
Group characteristics   Group characteristics

Coping mechanisms   Coping mechanisms

Capital market effects   Capital market effects

Solutions?

International standards   Reciprocity   Increased   Multiple
                                         disclosure   principles
                                                      capability

EXHIBIT 8
Matrix of Interview Candidates

LOCATION	NEW YORK	LONDON	ZURICH	FRANKFURT	TOKYO	Total
GROUPS						
BUYERS OF SECURITIES						
Large	3[a]	2	2	N.A.	2	9
Less large	2	1	3[b]	N.A.	2	8
SELLERS OF SECURITIES						
Large	2	2	1	2	2	9
Less large	2	2	N.A.	1	1	6
UNDERWRITERS	2[c]	2	N.A.	2	2	8
OTHERS						
Regulators, standards boards	1	1	1	N.A.	1	4
Exchange officials	1	1	1	1	1	5
Ratings agencies, data services	2	N.A.	N.A.	N.A.	1	3
Total	15	12	8	6	11	52

Note: [a] One interviewed in Tokyo office.

[b] One interviewed in New York and Zurich offices.

[c] One interviewed in London office.

N. A.: Not available.

BIBLIOGRAPHY

Ando, Albert, and Alan Auerbach. "The Cost of Capital in the U.S. and Japan: A Comparison." *NBER Working Paper No. 1762*, October 1985.

Ang, J. S., and R. A. Pohlman. "A Note on the Price Behavior of Far Eastern Stocks." *Journal of International Business Studies*, no. 1 (1978), pp. 103–7.

Aron, Paul. "Japanese P/E Multiples: The Tradition Continues." Daiwa Securities America, Inc., *Report #35*, October 23, 1989.

Ball, R. "Changes in Accounting Techniques and Stock Prices." *Empirical Research in Accounting, Selected Studies, 1972* (supplement), *Journal of Accounting Research* 10 (Spring 1972), pp. 1–38.

Ball, R., and P. Brown. "The Empirical Evaluation of Accounting Income Numbers." *Journal of Accounting Research*, Autumn 1968, pp. 159–77.

Barrett, M. Edgar. "Financial Reporting Practices: Disclosure and Comprehensiveness in an International Setting." *Journal of Accounting Research*, Spring 1976, pp. 10–26.

Beaver, W.; S. Kettler; and M. Scholes. "The Association between Market Determination and Accounting Determined Risk Measures." *Accounting Review*, October 1970, pp. 654–82.

Benston, George J. "Public (U.S.) Compared to Private (U.K.) Regulation of Corporate Financial Disclosure." *Accounting Review*, July 1976, pp. 483–98.

Bertoneche, M. "European Securities Markets: Efficiency, International Diversification and Prospects." Ph.D. dissertation, Northwestern University, 1978.

Branson, William H., and Dwight M. Jaffe. "The Globalization of Information and Capital Mobility." Working paper, Vincent C. Ross Institute of Accounting Research, New York University, September 15, 1989.

Brown, P., and J. W. Kennely. "The Information Content of Quarterly Earnings: An Extension and Further Evidence." *Journal of Business*, July 1972, pp. 403–15.

Brown, Stephen. "The Effect of Estimation Risk on Capital Market Equilibrium." *Journal of Financial and Quantitative Analysis* 14 (1979), pp. 215–20.

Castagna, A. D., and Z. P. Matolcsy. "A Two-stage Experimental Design to Test the Efficiency of the Market for Traded Stock Options and Australian Evidence." *Journal of Banking and Finance* 6, no. 4 (1982), pp. 521–32.

Castagna, A. D. and Z. P. Matolcsy. "The Evaluation of Traded Options Pricing Models in Australia." *Journal of Business, Finance and Accounting* 10, no. 2 (1983), pp. 225–33.

Choi, F. D. S. "Financial Disclosure in Relation to a Firm's Capital Costs." *Accounting and Business Research*, Autumn 1973, pp. 282–92.

————. "Financial Disclosure and Entry to the European Capital Market." *Journal of Accounting Research*, Autumn 1973b, pp. 159–75.

Choi, Frederick D. S.; Hisaaki Hino; Sang Kee Min; Sang Oh Nam; Junichi Ujiie; and Arthur Stonehill. "Analyzing Foreign Financial Statements: The Use and Misuse of International Ratio Analysis." *Journal of International Business Studies*, Spring/Summer 1983, pp. 113–31.

Choi, F. D. S., and S. B. Hong. "The Decision Utility of Restating Accounting Information Sets: Korea." In *Advances in Financial Planning and Forecasting*, ed. Raj Aggarwal, Greenwich, Conn.: JAI Press, forthcoming.

Choi, F. D. S. ; I. K. Joo; and Y. Kim. "The Information Content of Restated Accounting Numbers." Unpublished manuscript, New York University, January 1990.

Choi, F. D. S., and G. G. Mueller. *International Accounting*. Englewood Cliffs, N.J.: Prentice Hall, 1984.

Choi, Frederick D. S., and Joshua Ronen. "Financial Disclosure Policy in a Global Capital Market." *Proceedings of the Sixth International Conference on Accounting Education*. New York: Greenwood Press, 1988.

Collins, D. W. "SEC Product-Line Reporting and Market Efficiency." *Journal of Financial Economics II*, June 1975, pp. 125–64.

Conenberg, A., and E. Brandi. "The Information Content of Annual Accounting Income Numbers of German Corporations: A Review of German Accounting Standards and Some Preliminary Empirical Results." *Internationale Arbeitsberichte zur Betriebswirtschaftslehre der Universitat Augsburg*, no. 7, 1976.

Cumby, Robert E., and Jack D. Glen. "Evaluating the Performance of International Mutual Funds." *Journal of Finance*, June 1990.

D'Ambrosio, Charles A. "Random Walk and the Stock Exchange of Singapore." *Financial Review* 15, no. 2, 1980, pp. 1–9.

Dawson, Steven. "Is the Hongkong Market Efficient?" *Journal of Portfolio Management* 8, no. 3, 1981–82, pp. 10–16.

————. "The Trend Towards Efficiency for Less Developed Stock Exchanges: Hongkong." *Journal of Business, Finance and Accounting* 11, no. 2, 1984, pp. 151–61.

Dawson, Steven M. "Secondary Stock Market Performance of Initial Public Offerings: Hongkong, Singapore and Malaysia 1978–84." *Journal of Business, Finance and Accounting* 14, no. 1, 1987, pp. 65–76.

Deakin, Edward; Gyles Norwood; and Charles Smith. *International Journal of Accounting.* Fall 1974, pp. 123–36.

Dimson, Elroy, ed. *Stock Market Anomalies.* Cambridge: Cambridge University Press, 1988.

Dufey, Gunter. *The Eurobond Market: Function and Future.* Seattle: University of Washington Graduate School of Business, 1969.

Eun, Cheol S. and Bruce Resnick. "Estimating the Dependence Structure of Share Prices: A Comparative Study of the U.S. and Japan." *Financial Review* 23, no. 4, 1988, pp. 387–402.

Finn, Frank J., and Ron Higham, 1988. "The Performance of Unseasoned New Equity Issues-Cum-Stock Exchange Listings in Australia." *Journal of Banking and Finance* 12, no. 3, pp. 333–52.

Firth, M. "The Impact of Earnings Announcements on the Share Price Behavior of Similar Type Firms." *The Economic Journal*, June 1976, pp. 296–306.

Forsgardh, L. E., and K. Hertzen. "The Adjustment of Stock Prices to New Earnings Information: A Study of the Efficiency of the Swedish Stock Market." In *International Capital Markets.* eds. E. Elton and M. Gruber. Amsterdam: North-Holland Publishing Company, 1975.

Foster, T. W., and D. Vickrey. "The Information Content of Stock Dividend Announcements." *The Accounting Review*, April 1978, pp. 360–70.

Frankel, Jeffrey A. "Japanese Finance: A Survey." *NBER Working Paper No. 3156*, November 1989.

French, Kenneth, and James Poterba. "Are Japanese Stock Prices Too High?" Manuscript, NBER Summer Institute, August 1989.

Goldman Sachs International Limited. *Anatomy of World Markets.* London: Goldman Sachs, 1989.

Gonedes, N. "Capital Market Equilibrium and Annual Accounting Numbers: Empirical Evidence." *Journal of Accounting Research*, Spring 1976, pp. 89–137.

Grubel, Herbert G. "International Diversified Portfolios: Welfare Gains and Capital Flows." *American Economic Review* 58 (1968), pp. 1299–1314.

Gurwitz, Aaron S. "SEC Rule 144A and Regulation S: Impact on Global Fixed Income Markets." Fixed Income Research Series. New York: Goldman Sachs, September 1989.

Hamon, J. "Stock Price Forecasting and the Point and Figure Method: A Simulation Based on French Securities." *Analyse Financiere*, no. 22 (1975), pp. 24–37. (In French)

Hawawini, Gabriel. *European Equity Markets: Price Behavior and Efficiency.*

New York University Monograph Series in Finance and Economics, No. 1984–4/5, 1984.

Hong, H. "Predictability of Price Trends on Stock Exchanges: A Study of Some Far Eastern Countries." *Review of Economics and Statistics* 60, no. 4 (1978a), pp. 619–21.

――――. "The Random Walk in Stock Markets: Theory and Evidence." *Securities Industries Review* 4, no. 1, 1978b, pp. 25–29.

Hoshino, Yasuo. "The Performance of Corporate Mergers in Japan." *Journal of Business, Finance and Accounting* 9, no. 2, 1982, pp. 167–77.

Howell, Michael, and Angela Cozzini. *International Equity Flows: 1989 Edition*. London: Salomon Brothers, August 1989.

Hussein, M. "The Auditor's Report: Proposed IFAC Guideline and Current Worldwide Practices." Paper delivered at the annual meeting of the American Accounting Association, San Diego, California, 1982.

International Accounting Standards Committee. *Objectives and Procedures*. London: IASC, January 1983, par. 3; *Preface to Statements of International Accounting Standards*, par. 20.

Jaffe, Jeffrey, and Randolph Westerfield. "Patterns in Japanese Common Stock Returns: Day of the Week and Turn of the Year Effects." *Journal of Financial and Quantitative Analysis* 20, no. 2 (1985), pp. 261–72.

Jensen, Michael. "Organization Theory and Methodology." *Accounting Review* 58 (1983), pp. 319–39.

Jensen, Michael and W. Meckling. "Theory of the Firm: Managerial Behavior, Agency Costs and Ownership Structure." *Journal of Financial Economics* 3 (1976), pp. 305–60.

Kane, Edward J. "Competitive Financial Reregulation: An International Perspective." In *Threats to International Financial Stability*, ed. R. Portes and A. Swoboda, London: Cambridge University Press, 1987.

Kato, Kiyoshi, and James S. Schallheim. "Seasonal and Size Anomalies in the Japanese Stock Market." *Journal of Financial and Quantitative Analysis* 20, no. 2 (1985), pp. 243–60.

Kolb, Robert W. *Principles of Finance*. Glenview, Ill.: Scott, Foresman, 1988.

Korhonen, A. "Accounting Income Numbers, Information and Stock Prices: A Test of Market Efficiency." *The Finnish Journal of Business Economics* 24 (1975) pp. 306–22.

Kuroda, Akio. "Is the Japanese Bond Market Rational and Efficient." *Journal of Portfolio Management* 9, no. 1 (1982–83), pp. 46–51.

Lafferty, Michael. *World Accounting Survey*. London: Financial Times, 1980.

Lamberton, D. "Economic Growth and Stock Prices: The Australian Experience." *Journal of Business* 31, no. 3 (1958), pp. 200–212.

Larson, John C. and Joel N. Morse. "Intervailing effects in Hong Kong Stocks." *Journal of Financial Research* 10, no. 4 (1987), pp. 353–62.

Lau, Sheila C.; Stuart R. Quay; and Carl M. Ramsey. "The Tokyo Stock Exchange and the Capital Asset Pricing Model." *Journal of Finance* 29, no. 2 (1974), pp. 507–14.

Laurence, Martin M. "Weak Form Efficiency in the Kuala Lumpur and Singapore Stock Markets." *Journal of Banking and Finance* 10, no. 3 (1986), pp. 431–66.

LeRoy, Stephen F. "Efficient Capital Markets and Martingales." *Journal of Economic Literature* 27 (December 1989), pp. 1583–1621.

Lessard, Donald R. "World, Country, and Industry Relationships in Equity Returns: Implications for Risk Reduction Through International Diversification." *Financial Analysts Journal*, January–February 1976, pp. 2–8.

Levich, Richard M. "The Euromarkets after 1992." In *European Banking after 1992*, ed. Jean Dermine, London: Basil Blackwood, 1990.

Levich, Richard M., and Ingo Walter. "The Regulation of Global Financial Markets." In *New York's Financial Markets*, ed. T. Noyelle, Boulder, Colorado: Westview Press, 1989.

Levich, Richard M., and Ingo Walter. "Tax-Driven Regulatory Drag: European Financial Centers in the 1990s." New York University International Business Area *Working Paper, no. IB–90–1*, January 1990.

McDonald, J. G. "French Mutual Fund Performance: Evaluation of Internationally-Diversified Portfolios." *Journal of Finance*, December 1973, pp. 1160–80.

Maldonado-Bear, Rita, and Anthony Saunders. "Foreign Exchange Restrictions and the Law of One Price." *Financial Management* 12, no. 1 (Spring 1983), pp. 19–23.

Matolcsy, Z. P. "The Distributive Nominal and Real Micro Effects of Inflation on Security Returns: Some Australian Evidence." *Journal of Banking and Finance* 10, no. 3 (1985), pp. 326–465.

Meek, G. K., and S. J. Gray. "Globalization of Stock Markets and Foreign Listing Requirements: Voluntary Disclosures by Continental European Companies Listed on the London Stock Exchange." *Journal of International Business Studies* 20, no. 2 (Summer 1989), pp. 315–36.

National Association of Securities Dealers, Inc. *1989 NASDAQ Factbook*. Washington, D.C.: NASDAQ, 1989.

Nix, William E., and Susan W. Nix. *The Dow Jones-Irwin Guide to International Securities, Futures and Options Markets*. Homewood, Ill.: Dow Jones-Irwin, 1988.

Officer, R. R. "Seasonality in Australian Capital Markets: Market Efficiency and Empirical Issues." *Journal of Financial Economics* 2, no. 1 (1975), pp. 29–52.

Ooghe, H.; P. Beghin; and V. Verbaere. "The Efficiency of Capital Markets: A 'Semi-Strong Form' Test." *Tijdschriftvoor Economie en Management* 26 (1981), pp. 421–40.

Pagano, Marco, and Ailsa Roell. "Trading Systems in European Stock Exchanges: Current Performance and Policy Options." *Economic Policy*, April 1990.

Pettway, Richard H.; Tapley Craig; and Takeshi Yamada. "The Impact of Financial Deregulation upon Trading Efficiency and the Levels of Risk and Return of Japanese Banks." *Financial Review* 23, no. 3 (1988), pp. 243–68.

Pettway, Richard H., and Takeshi Yamada. "Mergers in Japan and Their Impacts upon Stockholders Wealth." *Financial Management* 15, no. 4 (1986), pp. 43–52.

Praetz. P.D. "Australian Share Prices and the Random Walk Hypothesis." *Australian Journal of Statistics* 11, (1969).

Ross, Stephen. "The Economic Theory of Agency: The Principal's Problem." *American Economic Review* 63 (1973), pp. 134–39.

Schineman, Gary S. "Japanese P/E Ratios: Are They Overstated by Conservative Accounting Practices?" Prudential Bache Securities, June 20, 1988.

————. "Japanese P/E Ratios II: Myth and Reality." Prudential Bache Securities, March 30, 1989.

Solnik, B.H. "Note on the Validity of the Random Walk for European Stock Prices." *Journal of Finance*, December 1973, pp. 1151–59.

Solnik, Bruno. *International Investments*. Reading, Mass.: Addison-Wesley Publishing, 1988.

Stamp, Edward, and Maurice Moonitz. "International Auditing Standards." *CPA Journal*, June 1982, pp. 24, 26, 28–30; July 1982, pp. 48–53.

Tandon, Kishore; Chris Hessel; and Nurset Cakici. "International Mergers and Acquisitions: Foreign Acquisitions in the U.S. and Effect on Shareholder Wealth." Stern School of Business Working Paper, New York University, December 1989.

UBS Philips & Drew. *Understanding European Financial Statements*. Basel: Union Bank of Switzerland, June 1987, pp. 4–5.

U.S. General Accounting Office. *International Finance: Regulation of International Securities Markets*. Washington, D.C.: GAO, April 1989.

Waller, David. "If Balance Sheets Don't Balance." *Financial Times*, January 30, 1990.

Walter, Ingo, and Roy C. Smith. *Investment Banking In Europe*. Oxford: Basil Blackwell, 1989.

APPENDIX 1

LIST OF ORGANIZATIONS INTERVIEWED

B.A.T. Industries, plc
Bank Julius Baer
Bear Stearns & Co., Inc.
BHF-Bank
Brown Brothers Harriman & Co.
Cadbury Schweppes, plc
Canon Inc.
Capital Research Co.
Deutsche Bank
Exxon Corporation
Federation of German Stock
 Exchanges
The Fuji Bank, Ltd.
General Electric Company
International Accounting Standards
 Board
Kleinwort Benson Ltd.
Lombard Odier & Cie.
London Stock Exchange
Merrill Lynch Asset Management
The Mitsubishi Trust and Banking
 Corp.
Moody's Investors Service
Morgan Grenfell Group, plc
Morval & Cie., S.A.
Nihon Keizai Shimbun Inc. (Data
 Bank Bureau)
Nestle, S.A.
New York Stock Exchange
Nippon Life Insurance Co.

Nissan Motor Company, Ltd.
Pfizer Inc.
Prudential-Bache
Prudential Portfolio Managers
 Limited
Reckitt & Colman, plc
SANYO Electric Co., Ltd.
Schering
Joseph E. Seagram & Sons, Inc.
Security Pacific Hoare Govett Ltd.
Siemens AG
Standard & Poor's Ratings Group
Swiss Bank Corporation
Swiss National Bank
Teachers Insurance Annuity
 Association–College Retirement
 Equity Fund
Tokyo Stock Exchange
Union Bank of Switzerland
Volkswagen AG
S.G. Warburg & Co., Ltd.
WPP Group, plc
Yamaichi Securities Company
Yamaichi Investment Trust
 Management
Zurich Stock Exchange
In addition, four organizations that
 wished to remain anonymous were
 interviewed.

APPENDIX 2

ADVANCE QUESTIONS FOR A SURVEY OF ATTITUDES REGARDING DIVERGENT ACCOUNTING PRINCIPLES AND GLOBAL CAPITAL MARKETS

This appendix contains the questionnaire and outline used for interviews with investors and fund managers. A similar questionnaire was used for interviews with issuers, underwriters, regulators, and rating agencies with suitable adjustments made for each of these respective groups.

New York University's Graduate School of Business Administration has received a seed grant from Arthur Andersen & Co. and Salomon Brothers, Inc. to begin a study of the effects of divergent accounting principles on global capital markets. Professors Frederick Choi and Richard Levich of the Graduate School of Business Administration are in charge of the research. The results of the study will be published and made available to interested parties. The contents of specific interviews will, of course, be held in confidence, and not even disclosed to the project sponsors.

STATEMENT OF PURPOSE

As a result of the globalization of the world's capital markets, financial decisions are increasingly international in scope. In contrast, financial statements are prepared in accordance with local practices and regulations, which may lead to problems in understanding and interpretation when the statements are used outside the home country. The juxtaposition of international financial decisions and divergent national accounting principles may have unfavorable consequences for capital market efficiency.

The purpose of this study is to determine how investors and issuers cope with the diversity in accounting principles around the world and to assess what impact, if any, this diversity has had on capital market decisions, the location of market activity and market growth.

In this phase of the study, we intend to gather information on the effects of financial reporting differences directly from capital market participants. We hope that these discussions will clarify the nature and scope of problems caused by accounting differences and thereby suggest a set of specific quantifiable relationships that will provide the basis for future inquiries.

INTRODUCTION TO THE QUESTIONNAIRE

The following questions will serve as a guide for the nature of the issues we would like to discuss with you and appropriate representatives of your firm. In some cases, we have supplied a set of possible responses to indicate the type of issues we would like you to address. However, these responses are merely suggestive and we intend to cover these questions in more depth during the interview.

The capital market decisions of portfolio managers who invest in securities and corporate treasurers who issue securities are made within the context of advice offered by underwriting firms (investment bankers) and guidelines enforced by national regulators. For each of these users of accounting information, we wish to explore a variety of issues that may be grouped under the following headings:

Part I.   Background Profile of Users

Part II.   Nature of Decisions Faced by Users of Accounting Information

Part III. Information Requirements for Decision Making

Part IV.   The Nature of Accounting Diversity

Part V.   Coping with Accounting Diversity

Part VI.   Capital Market Effects of Accounting Diversity

Part VII. Future Directions

QUESTIONS FOR INVESTORS/FUNDS MANAGERS

Part I.   Background Profile of Users
A. Obtain background information (e.g., an Annual Report) in advance of the interview.
B. Job description of respondent
1. Title and decision responsibilities of respondent? (Note: Respondent must have responsibility for making "international choices," that is, allocating portfolio investments *between* the home and foreign countries, or *among* foreign countries.)
2. Where is respondent in reporting chain of command?
3. Who is responsible for making the investment decisions?
C. Do you now invest internationally?
1. Yes—When did you make your first international investment?
a. In how many countries do you hold investments?
b. How large are these international positions?
c. Nature of instruments held—bonds (maturities, special features), equities?
d. How many foreign countries do you monitor for possible investments?
2. No—Why are foreign securities not part of your investment portfolio?

Part II.   Nature of Decisions Faced by Users of Accounting Information
A. Describe your general investment philosophy and objectives. (E.g., outperform the market [national market, world market]. Find undervalued, counter-cyclical stocks. Match the market, diversification gains. Expand funds under management.)
B. Describe the scope of the investment choices that you make. (E.g., selection of country, industry, firm, currency of denomination, amount of investment, hedge/ don't hedge currency component of investment, buy/sell.)
1. Under what investment constraints do you operate?
C. How are comparisons made between alternative investment opportunities?

1. Do you select country weights and then select individual stocks within that country?
2. Do you select stocks without regard to their country of domicile?
3. How do you choose between home country and host country investments?
4. How do you choose between investments in one foreign country and another foreign country?

D. In making your investment decisions, what variables do you consider? (E.g., do you compute indicators such as expected returns, price/earnings and other financial ratios, risk measures, cash flow, etc.)
1. Do you use a specific model for decision making?

Part III. Information Requirements for Decision Making
A. What role do the following classes of information play in your analysis?
1. Market parameters (prospects for P/E ratios, interest rate levels, market over- or undervaluation, others).
2. Firm-specific factors (prospects for earnings, sales, market share, new products, name recognition, special situations, financial statements, others).
3. Macroeconomic (national GNP, interest rates, savings rate, FX volatility, trade balance, fiscal deficit, terms of trade, others).
4. Political (president in office, party in office, political unrest, country risk ratings, others).
5. Regulatory (present or pending restrictions [for example, only nonvoting shares available to non-resident investors, currency restrictions]).
6. Taxes

Part IV. The Nature of Accounting Diversity
A. What does the term *accounting diversity* mean to you?
1. Differences in measurement rules (i.e., accounting principles, regulatory accounting principles, tax accounting principles)?
2. Differences in financial disclosure?
3. Differences in auditing standards and procedures?
4. Other?

B. Is accounting diversity as you have defined it important to you?
   1. If so, why is it important?
      a. Measurement principles.
      b. Disclosure practices.
      c. Auditing principles and practices.
   2. If not, why not?
C. Accounting principles
   1. Is the measurement of your decision variables hindered by the absence of comparable accounting standards, i.e., measurement rules?
   2. For which countries are differences in accounting principles most problematic?
   3. For the countries you mentioned, which *industries* are most difficult for you?

   Following is a list of items where differences in national accounting measurements may raise problems for the user of accounting information. For the measurements which play a key role in your decision process, which country differences raise the most problems for you?

   Blocked accounts
   Provision for bad debts
   Long-term construction contracts
   Marketable securities
   Inventory valuation
   Overhead allocations to inventory
   Lower of cost or market rule
   Long-term investments; e.g., cost versus equity
   Consolidated accounts
   Valuation of fixed assets
   Depreciation methods
   Excess depreciation
   Business combinations; e.g. pooling versus purchase
   Amortization of goodwill
   R&D expenditures
   Bond discount/premium

Deferred taxes
Leases
Pension costs
Treasury stock
Discretionary reserves
Severance indemnities
Minority interest
Price level adjustments
Foreign currency transaction gains/losses
Foreign currency translation method
Foreign currency translation gains/losses
Stock dividends
Revenue recognition
Contingencies
Other

D. Financial Disclosure
1. Is the measurement of your decision variables hindered by the absence of comparable standards of corporate financial disclosure?
2. For which countries are disclosure differences most pronounced?
3. Following is a list of disclosure items where difference in national practices may raise problems for the user of accounting information.
For the disclosure items which play a key role in your decision process, which country-differences raise the most problems for you?

Comparative financial statements
Frequency and completeness of interim information
Funds flow statement
Time series data on financial statistics
Method of asset valuation
Details of financial statement items
Location of data
Segmental disclosures
Foreign operations disclosures
Description of capital expenditures
Research expenditures

Major factors affecting future business
Labor contracts
Management objectives and policies
Accounting policies
Details of capital structure
Discussion of new product development
Discussion of industry trends
Description of management
Off-balance sheet disclosures
Financial forecasts
Value-added statements
Auditor's report
Pending litigation
Related party transactions
Social responsibility disclosures
Other
E. Auditing Practices
1. Is the measurement of your decision variables hindered by national audit differences? (E.g., credibility of auditor's attestations.)
2. For which countries are audit differences most pronounced?
3. Following is a list of audit items for which differences in national practice may raise problems for the user of accounting information.
Which of the following audit differences confront you with the greatest problems in your decision process?

Confirmation of receivables and payables
Observation of physical inventory counts
Auditor qualifications
Auditor independence
Other
Part V.   Coping with Accounting Diversity
A. Do you attempt to deal with differences in accounting principles?
1. Yes
How is this accomplished?
Are "restated" accounting figures used?

What is the source of restated figures?
What figures are restated?
What method is used to restate?
How much confidence is placed on the restated data?
If you do not restate, what do you do?
2. No
Why not?
B. If GAAP restatements are performed, how are restated accounting figures used?
1. To make comparisons with other investment opportunities?
2. To make comparisons with in-house benchmarks/guidelines?
C. Are some comparisons of restated accounting figures with comparable figures for other investment opportunities
1. Difficult to make?
2. Imperfect? More imperfect than with other cases?
D. Do you attempt to deal with financial disclosure differences?
1. If so, how is this accomplished?
2. If not, why not?
E. Do you attempt to deal with auditing differences?
1. If so, how is this accomplished?
2. If not, why not?
Part VI. Capital Market Effects of Accounting Diversity
A. How does accounting diversity affect your investment decision process?
1. With respect to the geographic location of your investments?
2. With respect to the types of securities you invest in?
3. With respect to the types of companies you invest in?
B. Do you attempt to reduce the diversity of the accounting information that you process in order to arrive at your investment decisions?
If yes, at what cost?
If no, then do you adjust your break-even decision points?
(That is, do you require more overwhelming accounting evidence [i.e., require a higher return on investment] to

buy a foreign security, or a security in a foreign market, than for a "comparable" domestic security?)

C. Do you refuse to consider investments in firms that follow a particular accounting method?

D. Do differences in accounting principles affect your valuation of securities?
1. If so, how is this effect manifested?
2. If not, why not?

E. Do differences in financial disclosure affect your valuation of securities?
1. If so, how is this effect manifested?
2. If not, why not?

F. Do differences in auditing principles and practices affect your valuation of securities?
1. If so, how is this effect manifested?
2. If not, why not?

Part VII. Future Directions

A. Are you planning to increase your investments in the future?
1. Yes
a. What are the motivating factors?
b. What preconditions are necessary to encourage you to increase your investments abroad?
2. No
a. What are the reasons for your position?
b. What preconditions would entice you to change your behavior?

INDEX